The Private Pilot Flying Course

Author: John Pullen

Copyright © 2012 John Pullen

Publisher: John Pullen

First Print Edition: 2015

Printed by CreateSpace, An Amazon.com Company

Cover Image Design: JPP

Available from Amazon.com, CreateSpace.com and other
retail outlets

www.johnpullenwriter.com

For

All pilots everywhere who are flying their dream

Contents

Chapter 4

10

The Powered Descent

Use of Flap in the Descent

The Sideslip

Chapter 12

The Medium Level Turn

The Climbing Turn

Descending Turns

The Gliding Turn

The Descending Turn Using Power

Descending Turns with Flap Extended

Sideslipping in a Descending Turn

Turning onto Selected Headings

Using the Direction Indicator

Using the Turn Co-Ordinator and Clock

Using the Magnetic Compass

Chapter 13

Stall Recovery Using Power

Stall Recovery Without Using Power

Chapter 14

Chapter 15

Full Spins

Incipient Spins

Chapter 16

Engine Failure After Take-Off

Discontinued Take-Off

Chapter 17

Circuit, Powered Approach & Normal Landing

The Go-Around

Departing & Joining the Circuit

The Flapless Approach & Landing

13

Nose High/Low Airspeed

Nose Low/High Airspeed

Steep Descending Turns

Chapter 24

Using the Flight Instruments   **182**

Flying Straight & Level on Instruments

Establishing Straight & Level Flight

Raising the Nose at Constant Power

Lowering the Nose at Constant Power

Maintaining Straight & Level Flight at Constant Power

Changing Airspeed in Straight & Level Flight

Climbing, Cruising and Descending at Constant Power

Climb, Cruise & Descend at Constant Airspeed

Initiating a Climb at Normal Climb Speed

Levelling Off from a Climb

Initiating a Descent on Instruments

Controlling the Rate of Descent at a Constant Airspeed

Levelling Off from a Descent

Climbing Away from a Descent

Turning Using the Flight Instruments

The Rate 1 Turn

The 30 Degree Banked Level Turn

The Climbing Turn

Descending Turns

Recovery from Unusual Attitudes

Nose High/Steep Bank

Nose Low/Steep Bank

Author

Pilot Training Aids

Other Books by the Author

.

Introduction

Many dream of becoming a pilot but few realise it in their life. Most people can be taught to fly but for those who have taken the first steps towards the coveted pilot's licence, they will be only too aware that it does take hard work and application to achieve their ambition.

There is a medical to pass, a number of groundwork courses and exams to take and then there is the flying course itself with its own tests and exams at the end. This book aims to cover in a clear and concise way the whole of the flying course – from checklists, ground inspections, take-off, flight manoeuvres, navigation, flying on instruments and finally making a safe landing under various conditions.

The exercises cover the entire flying course for the private pilot's licence and students following either the European EASA course or Americans studying the FAA course will find this guide a useful aid.

Use as a training aid and a reference source

It is recommended that a student should study a particular exercise in the book before practising it for real with their instructor in the aircraft. In that way the fundamentals and procedures will have been learnt allowing the time in the cockpit to be devoted to flying the manoeuvre. This should help the student pilot to save both time and money.

This book can also be used as a reference source by qualified pilots just before taking their periodical re-tests and check flights.

Flying is a wonderful hobby or occupation – enjoy every flight.

Chapter 1

Emergency Checklists

It may at first seem a bit strange to begin a book on flying a plane by describing a series of checklists that will only be used in an emergency. But if you think about it, an emergency, although very rare, can occur at any time during a flight. And if you are new to learning to fly or if your first lesson in the air is approaching, then you should be prepared.

Although much of your training is spent in the company of your flying instructor and he or she will direct you if a problem should arise, it is better to be prepared to act in the correct way. An urban legend from military flight training perhaps sums up unpreparedness best of all; instructor to student, "If I say Eject and you say "Pardon" you'll be talking to yourself."

So let's start. The first thing to remember is that emergencies don't just happen in the air; they can occur on the ground as well and some involve fire.

Engine Fire at Start-Up

If possible keep the engine turning over with the starter and move the Mixture Control to IDLE CUT-OFF. If there is a Fuel Selector, switch it to OFF. This will starve the engine of fuel and the fire should extinguish itself.

If not, then;-

Fuel: OFF

Switches: OFF

Brakes: ON

Then evacuate the aircraft taking the Fire Extinguisher with you.

Engine Fire in Flight

A probable cause for an engine fire in flight is either fuel or oil leaking under pressure. The procedure is;-

Throttle: CLOSED

Fuel Selector: OFF

Mixture: IDLE CUT-OFF

Ignition Switches: OFF

Cabin Heat: OFF (this is done to avoid fumes coming into the cabin)

In cases of fire in the air, remember to fly the aircraft and maintain a safe flying speed. Then you should follow the procedure for a Forced Landing.

Electrical Fire

An electrical fire has a very distinct smell, so if you suspect one;-

Master Switch: OFF

All Other Switches (except Ignition): OFF

Cabin Heat: OFF

Cabin Vent: As Advised for your Aircraft

Fire Extinguisher: Use as Needed

On the Ground:

Shut down the engine and Evacuate the aircraft taking the Fire Extinguisher with you.

In the Air:

If possible, keep the engine running and make a landing as soon as possible. If you do have to shut the engine down, follow the Forced Landing procedure.

Cabin Fire

First identify where the fire is coming from and use the extinguisher as required.

<u>On the Ground</u>

Shut-Down the Engine

Fuel Selector: OFF

Mixture: IDLE CUT-OFF

Switches: OFF

Brakes: ON

Evacuate the Aircraft

Use the Fire Extinguisher as required

<u>In the Air</u>

Use the Fire Extinguisher as required

Ventilate the cabin to avoid fumes

Remember to Fly the Aircraft

Decide whether a Forced Landing is necessary

Brake Failure

If a brake failure occurs whilst taxiing the aircraft;-

Throttle: CLOSED

(Shut-Down the Engine if required)

Keep Clear of Obstacles

If a collision is likely;-

Fuel Selector: OFF

Mixture: IDLE CUT-OFF

Ignition: OFF

Master Switch: OFF

These then are the basics of what to do in an emergency situation. The checklists should be memorised as time will not normally permit you to consult your checklist. But remember to check for any differences in procedures affecting your particular aircraft or the rules applying to your Flying Organisation.

If in doubt, always consult your flying instructor.

Chapter 2

External Inspection

Introduction

Each stage of any flight will necessitate the need to consult checklists. This applies to a single engine aircraft on a short pleasure flight or to an airliner beginning a long-haul journey across the world. They are there for a reason; so that the pilot or aircrew do not miss out a vitally important check or action in the cockpit.

Some checklists such as the emergency ones in the last chapter should be memorised, but it is good airmanship to always consult each list no matter how many times you have done so in the past. It only requires one error or omission to make things difficult.

So let's start with the first one you should consult when you approach your aircraft; the external inspection. However, before you carry out your external inspection, you should have also checked all the aircraft's documentation in order to make sure that it is mechanically sound and legal to fly. Also, make sure that your personal documents are in order and that you are current on type.

Use the approved checklist for your aircraft

The following list has to be a general one which will apply to most aircraft. But remember to always use the lists for your particular aircraft which can be found in your Pilot's Operating Handbook. If you have any doubts about any checklists, consult your instructor or your Flight Training Organisation.

The Walk-Around

On arrival at your aircraft, you should first ensure that the;-

Brakes are ON

Magneto Switches are OFF

Control Locks are REMOVED

Flaps are LOWERED for inspection

Doors can be LATCHED.

Do not trust your fuel gauges. Instead, check each tank visually. Use a measuring rod for your particular aircraft and always allow enough extra fuel so that you can divert to another airport if you have to. Drain a little fuel out of each tank and ensure that it is not contaminated.

Water is usually the culprit and since it is denser than fuel, it will be seen to collect at the bottom of your drainer. Also check for any sediment in the fuel and that its colour is the correct one for your type of fuel. Once you are satisfied, carefully replace the fuel caps.

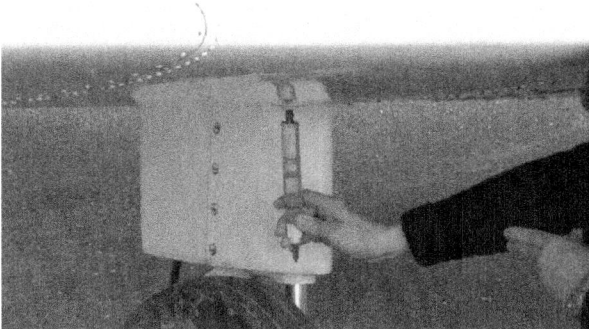

Drain off some fuel to check for contamination

Next check the Static Vents and Pitot Tube to make sure they are clear.

This is especially important in the case of the Pitot Tube when flying in the summer months. Insects can get inside and block the airflow. This can result in your Airspeed Indicator (ASI) giving a low false reading which can be dangerous.

A blocked Static Vent will affect your other pressure instruments.

Walk along the leading edge of the wing and check that it is undamaged and that there are no build ups of dead insects or dirt present as these can affect the airflow over the wing causing a loss of lift and performance.

Make sure the leading edge is clean and undamaged

At the tips of the wings, check the Wingtip and Navigation lights for damage.

Check the Ailerons for full and correct movement; as one goes Up, the one on the opposite wing goes Down.

Now check the Flap Hinge mechanism to make sure it is secure and that there is no wrinkled skin.

Check the flap hinge mechanism is secure

As you reach the undercarriage, check the tyres for correct inflation. Carefully inspect them for any defects and remember to check the Creep Mark to ensure the tyre has not slipped.

Whilst you are there, check the Hydraulic Lines going to the brakes and ensure there are no leaks. Then check that the Brake Disc itself is secure.

Finally, make sure there is no damage to the Landing Gear Strut which could have resulted from a previous heavy landing.

As you walk around the aircraft, continually look at all the surfaces for signs of damage; any popped rivets, wrinkling or buckling of the surface skin. If you find any defects, report it before you go flying.

When you reach the aft end of the aircraft begin your inspection of the Tail-Plane. Check that the structure feels secure and that the control surfaces give full and free movement. This will include both the Elevators and Rudder. Carefully check that all the locking pins are in place and do the same for the Trim Tab.

Check the locking pins are all in place

At this stage, you will have completed one side of the aircraft. But you have two sides and two wings, so repeat the procedure just as carefully on the other side.

You've now completed your checks of both sides and the aft end of the aircraft. You are now at the front where your powerplant or engine is situated. Go to the propeller and check for any nicks or cracks. This is especially important along the leading edge and at the tips.

Check the propeller for nicks and cracks

Behind the propeller you should find the engine intake and filter, so make sure that they are clear of any blockages. If it is accessible, check inside the engine compartment for any broken or loose cables and that there are no cracks in the manifold.

Now check the Oil Level. There is a Dipstick which is similar to the types found in car engines. However, ensure the aircraft is parked on level ground so that the reading will be an accurate one. Once you have finished make sure that the dipstick is replaced and that the Inspection Covers are secured correctly.

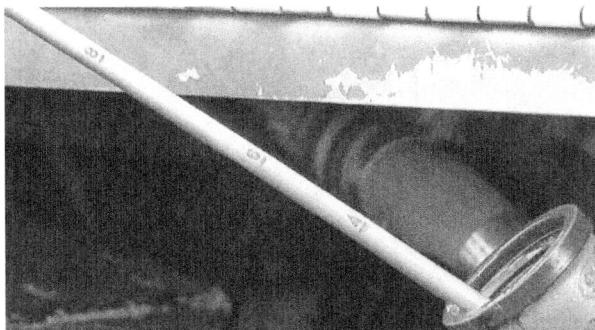

Check you have sufficient oil

It's now time to check the Nose-Wheel assembly. First, make sure the Oleo Strut extends properly. For many aircraft, this is about 5 centimetres. Check for any fluid leakages. Then make sure the Shimmy Dampener is secure. Finally check the tyre for correct inflation and that the creep mark has not slipped.

Only when satisfied should you begin your internal inspection

You're now coming to the end of the external inspection so stand back and just check that the windscreen looks clean, that there are no

35

broken aerials you may have missed and that all the Tie-Downs and Wheel-Chocks have been removed. Once satisfied, you can get ready to enter the aircraft and begin your Internal Inspection.

Chapter 3

Internal Inspection

The same warning applies to the Internal Inspection checklists as it did to the External one; these are generic checklists.

Always refer to the one designed for your particular aircraft.

This will be found in your Pilot's Operating Handbook or as a separate document provided by your Flight Training Organisation.

The following Checklists will take us through the initial inspection of the cockpit and engine start up.

Internal Checklist

This list will take you from entering the aircraft to starting the engine.

Seat: Adjusted Correctly

Harness ON

Brakes: ON

First Aid Kit: Checked and in place

Fire Extinguisher: In place and Serviceable

Fuel: ON

Master Switch: ON

Fuel Gauges: Rising

Circuit Breakers: All In

Cabin Air: Set Closed

Flaps: Operate and Leave Up

Mixture: Fully Rich

Throttle Nut: Finger Tight

Carb Heat: Set Cold

Controls: Full and Free Travel

Trim: Check Travel and Set for Take-Off

Instruments: No Broken or Cracked Glass

Radio: OFF

Beacon: ON

Starter Key: Insert

Primer: Prime as Required

Fuel Pump (if fitted): ON

Engine: Look Out. Shout "Clear Prop." Start Engine as required.

Call "clear prop" before starting the engine

After Starting Checklist

As the engine starts, go through the following checks;-

Tachometer: Set to 1,000 rpm or as required

Oil Pressure: Check. If not in the GREEN ARC in 30 seconds, SHUT DOWN ENGINE

Temperature Gauge: Rising towards the GREEN ARC

Ammeter: Charging (giving a positive reading)

Suction: Available

Magnetos: Check Live or Dead

Instruments: Set as Required

Radio: Select Frequency. Obtain Radio Check and Airfield Information.

Chapter 4

Flying Controls

Introduction

In the vast majority of aircraft you are likely to encounter, there are 3 main flying controls;-

Elevators

Ailerons

Rudder

The use of each of them produces a primary effect or movement of the aircraft. There is also an associated secondary effect with each of them. We will look at both of these effects in due course.

The attitude of an aircraft can be expressed in terms of 3 axes passing through its centre of gravity (C of G) and an aircraft can be moved about each of these axes by using the flying controls.

Elevators

The first axis is called the Lateral Axis and can be imagined as a line stretching across both wings (say from wing tip to wing tip). A movement around this axis will result in the nose moving up or down. This is called Pitching and pitching is caused by the pilot pulling or pushing the control column back or forward.

This action causes the elevators, located horizontally on the tail of the aircraft, to move up or down.

If they move up, the nose pitches up.

If they move down, the nose pitches down.

Lateral Axis

Ailerons

The second axis is called the Longitudinal Axis and it can be imagined as a line running from the nose of the aircraft to the tail. A movement around this axis will cause the plane to Roll and rolling happens when the pilot moves the control column to the left or right.

This action causes the ailerons, which are usually located on the trailing edge of the wings near the wing tips, to either move up or down. However, what is important to note, is that if one aileron goes up, the one on the opposite wing will go down and vice-versa.

Therefore, if the pilot moves the control column to the left;-

the Left aileron goes up and the Right aileron goes down.

The effect of this is;-

the Left wing goes down and the Right wing goes up.

The result;-

the plane rolls to the Left.

Longitudinal Axis

Rudder

The final axis is called the Normal Axis and can be imagined as a line passing vertically (from top to bottom) through the aircraft's centre of gravity. A movement around this axis will cause the plane to Yaw either to the left or right. This will happen when the pilot depresses either the left or right rudder pedal.

This action causes the rudder, which is located vertically along the trailing edge of the tail, to move to the left or right.

If the pilot depresses the Left rudder pedal;-

the rudder moves to the Left and

the aircraft yaws to the Left.

If the pilot depresses the Right rudder pedal;-

the rudder moves to the Right and

the aircraft yaws to the Right.

That concludes the Introduction on how we can control an aircraft. We will now take a more detailed look at the primary effects of each of the main controls.

Normal Axis

Primary Effect of the Flying Controls

Just to recap, there are 3 main flight controls;-

Elevators

Ailerons

Rudder

Each of them has a primary effect on an aircraft's movement and they are each controlled by the pilot.

From now on, to help you understand how to fly a plane up to the standard of a Private Pilot, you will imagine that you are sitting in the cockpit as the student pilot and I will take you through each Flight Exercise.

By adopting this approach, when you practice each exercise for real, it will feel familiar to you.

Okay, so you're flying your aircraft in straight and level flight. Always remember to keep a good look out for other traffic.

Throughout, you will hear me repeat instructions such as this. These are things you must make a part of your flying skills at all times; they should become second nature to you and will indicate that you are displaying a high level of good airmanship.

Elevators

The primary effect of the elevators is to pitch the aircraft up or down. When demonstrating most flight exercises, the aircraft is first set up in balance with the attitude being Straight and Level. To achieve this balance and flying an aircraft in straight and level flight will be discussed later.

The elevators cause the aircraft to pitch up & down

To demonstrate the primary effect of the elevators, first smoothly and gently move the control column forwards. The nose pitches down and you can see this by a change in the horizon in front of you; it has moved up the windshield.

Hold this new attitude and look at your Airspeed Indicator. It is increasing.

Now, smoothly and gently move the control column towards you and notice that the nose pitches up. Hold this new attitude and observe that your airspeed is now decreasing. This is the primary effect of the elevators.

Control Column Forward – Nose Pitches Down – Airspeed Increases

Control Column Back – Nose Pitches Up – Airspeed Decreases

Ailerons

We'll now look at the primary effect of using the ailerons. So once again imagine you are in the cockpit and you have the aircraft flying straight and level and in balance. Keep a good look out.

The ailerons cause the aircraft to roll left or right

Now, smoothly and gently turn the control column to the left and notice that the aircraft rolls to the left.

Then centre the control column and observe that the roll stops and that the aircraft continues at the same angle of bank.

To return to straight and level flight, simply rotate the control column this time, to the right. The aircraft now begins to roll to the right.

When the wings become level, centralise the control column again. The roll stops and you are back in straight and level flight. If you are slightly out, make small adjustments until you get back to straight and level.

As part of your training, you will practice this manoeuvre for both left and right turns.

Rudder

Finally, we shall investigate the primary effect of using the rudder. And the primary effect of the rudder is to yaw the aircraft.

To demonstrate this, once again imagine you are in straight and level flight with the aircraft in balance.

First, select a reference point on the horizon. Next smoothly and gently apply some left rudder. The nose of the aircraft will yaw to the left. For confirmation, look at the Ball within the Turn Co-Ordinator and notice that it has moved over to the right.

Now centralise the rudder pedals and notice that the aircraft returns to its original attitude. Remember to practice this manoeuvre by yawing to both the left and right.

It is also important to note that the same primary effects apply to the aircraft even if it is not flying straight and level. So practice these exercises whilst in turns to the right and left.

That covers the primary effects of the main flying controls. In the next section, we shall explore the secondary effects of these flight controls.

Secondary Effects of the Flying Controls

Introduction

In the previous section we saw that there is a primary effect from using each of our main flight controls.

But there are also secondary effects and these other effects can complicate our flying. So we must be aware of them and take them into account.

For example, using the aileron causes the aircraft to roll. But it also has the effect of causing the aircraft to yaw.

Using the rudder has the primary effect of yawing the aircraft. But it also produces roll.

Finally, if you use the elevators, the aircraft will change its pitch. But it also has the secondary effect of altering the airspeed.

Let's look at each in turn.

Ailerons

We will now demonstrate the secondary effect of ailerons which is yaw.

You are flying the aircraft which is in straight and level flight and in balance.

First, take your feet off the rudder pedals.

Now gently move the control column to the left. The plane begins to roll to the left.

But also notice that this causes sideslip. The aircraft is yawing towards the lower left wing. You can see this happening because the nose of the aircraft is dropping.

A left turn also causes a yaw to the left

Take a few moments to visualise clearly these effects on the aircraft before moving on.

Rudder

In this example, we're going to demonstrate the secondary effect of using the rudder, which is to roll the aircraft.

Once again, set the aircraft up in straight and level flight. It must also be in balance.

Now, take your hands off the control column and then apply some left rudder.

The aircraft first yaws to the left as we would expect, but then begins to roll, also to the left.

A yaw also causes a roll in the same direction

Again, spend some moments getting a clear picture in your mind of how the aircraft reacts.

Finally, we shall look at the secondary effects of using the elevators.

Elevators

We already know that the primary effect of using the elevators is to change the pitch of the aircraft. However, the secondary effect is to also alter our airspeed. Let's take a look.

Set the aircraft up in straight and level flight and in balance.

Next, ease the control column forwards. The nose pitches down and you can see this through the windscreen by the horizon moving up.

Now, check your airspeed indicator. It will be increasing.

A change of pitch also causes a change in airspeed

To recover, ease the control column back and you will notice that the nose of the aircraft pitches up. Look again at the airspeed indicator. This time it will be decreasing.

It is important to bear in mind that these effects will be present even if the aircraft is in another attitude such as climbing, banking or descending.

That concludes our look at the secondary effects of the main flying controls. In the next part, we will see how to Trim the aircraft.

Trimming the Aircraft

If you can understand trimming and apply it correctly to the aircraft, then your flying will become easier and less strenuous.

The Trim Control is used to reduce the prolonged pressure you may experience on the control column. This pressure may be caused by;-

a change in pitch,

the power level selected,

your flap setting or

a change in the aircraft's centre of gravity.

To demonstrate how to trim an aircraft, imagine that you are in straight and level flight and that you are also in balance.

Now, push the throttle forward to increase power and ease the control column forward to maintain your present height. The airspeed will increase and as it does, the pressure on the control column will also increase. The aircraft wants to climb and you have to use more and more strength to keep the control column pushed forward. This will become very tiring over time.

Therefore to relieve the pressure, place your hand on the Trim Wheel (or operate the Electric Trim if fitted) and rotate it forwards. Notice that the pressure begins to slacken off and when you can feel no more pressure, let go of the control column.

If the aircraft has been trimmed correctly, you should be able to continue flying at the same pitch angle.

Correct trimming takes pressure off the control column

You should practice trimming the aircraft in other attitudes. After a while, it will become second nature and this will allow you to concentrate on your other flying responsibilities.

Over the next few sections we are going to consider the effect of other factors on our main flying controls. The first factors we shall consider are Airspeed and Slipstream.

Effect of Airspeed & Slipstream on the Flying Controls

Introduction

We are now going to look at the effect that Airspeed and Slipstream have on our main flying controls. The effectiveness of each of the main flying controls depends on 3 factors;-

the amount of deflection,

the airspeed and

the slipstream generated by the propeller.

The greater the airspeed, the more effective each of the controls become and therefore, deflections can be correspondingly smaller.

At low airspeeds, the controls will feel "sloppy" and therefore greater deflections will be necessary.

The slipstream which is produced by the propeller only influences the elevators and rudder.

The ailerons which are located on the trailing edge of the wings close to the wingtips will be outside of the slipstream and therefore unaffected. So an increase in slipstream without an increase in airspeed will only improve the "feel" of the elevators and rudder.

Another factor to consider is that increasing the slipstream also causes an increase in yaw. The direction (left or right) of the yaw will depend on the direction of rotation of your particular propeller.

Effect of Airspeed

Okay, let's demonstrate the effect of airspeed on the main flying controls.

So imagine once again, you are flying your aircraft straight and level and in balance. Don't forget to keep a good look out.

For this exercise, we need to limit the effect of the slipstream. Therefore, we are going to put the aircraft in a glide. So check that your mixture is rich and select carburettor heat.

Now, close the throttle.

You need to maintain a fairly high airspeed, so gently ease the control column forward.

Now, operate the main flying controls and notice that they feel firm. It only requires a small input from you the pilot, to get a strong response from the aircraft.

Next ease back gently on the control column and let your airspeed bleed back to a slower speed. Notice now how each of the main flying controls feel more "sloppy" and require much larger deflections in order to produce the same response.

Let's now look at the effect of slipstream.

Effect of Slipstream

For us to demonstrate the effect of slipstream, we must establish the aircraft in straight and level flight.

But this time, the aircraft must also be in slow flight. The procedures of slow flight will be covered in a future section.

Now, apply climb power and raise the nose in order to maintain the same slow airspeed. The slipstream produced by the propeller has increased and this will be noticed by the firmer feel of the elevators and rudder. Their responsiveness has increased.

However, the ailerons, which are outside of the slipstream, still feel "sloppy" and unresponsive.

In the next section, we will examine the effect of power changes on the main flying controls.

Effect of Power Changes on the Flying Controls

Introduction

Continuing our look at the different factors that influence the main flying controls of an aircraft in flight, we will now consider the effect of making changes in engine power.

Power changes will cause an aircraft to alter its pitch and to yaw.

Increase power and the nose will pitch up and if the propeller is a clockwise rotating propeller, it will cause the aircraft to yaw to the left.

Decrease power and the nose will pitch down and if the propeller rotates in a clockwise direction, the aircraft will yaw in the opposite direction.

Effect of Power Changes

To demonstrate the effect of making changes to power, imagine that you are flying the plane, so first establish the aircraft in straight and level flight and in balance. Remember always to keep a good look out.

Now take your hands off the control column and your feet off the rudder pedals.

Next, smoothly and gently, open up the throttle to full power.

The nose of the aircraft pitches up and you can see this as the horizon getting lower in the windscreen. But you also notice that the aircraft is yawing to the left (we are assuming your propeller rotates in a clockwise direction).

Now, close the throttle and notice that the nose begins to pitch down allowing you to see more of the ground through the windscreen.

But in addition, you also notice that the aircraft is now yawing in the opposite direction; in other words, to the right.

This has been a short section but these effects will be experienced many times during a flight, so understand them and practice them.

In the next section, we will consider the effect of using flaps which is a little more involved.

Effect of Using Flaps

Introduction

Using flaps cause a number of effects in the handling of an aircraft in flight. For example, they have the effect of changing the shape of the wing and this will have an effect on both your Lift and Drag.

Flaps are also used to;-

generate lift at lower airspeeds

steepen the descent before landing and

improve forward vision as the nose will now be lower.

Safe flap operation range is shown as the white arc

The Flap Operation Range can be seen as the White Arc on the Airspeed Indicator. The low end of the arc indicates at what speed that particular aircraft will stall with full flap and at maximum weight.

Let's now look at each of the effects in turn.

Changing Flap Causes Pitching

First imagine that your aircraft in set up in the usual way; in balance and flying straight and level. At this point you have deployed no flap, so your flap setting is zero.

Now look at the Airspeed Indicator and make sure your airspeed is within the white arc. This means that you are flying slow enough to lower your flaps safely.

Next remove your hands from the control column and lower the flap in stages.

Lowering flap caused the aircraft to pitch up

The aircraft will tend to "balloon" and pitch up. To compensate, push the control column forwards and re-trim the aircraft for straight and level flight.

Okay, once you have achieved this, again remove your hands from the control column and this time, raise the flap in stages.

Notice that the aircraft now pitches down and that there is a loss of height.

Raising flap causes the aircraft to pitch down

We'll now move on to the effect on Lift and Drag.

Flaps Increase Lift and Drag

We are now going to demonstrate that flaps increase both lift and drag. So establish the aircraft in straight and level flight and with no flap deployed. Do not touch the throttle during this exercise.

Now, lower the first stage of flap. Hold the pitch of the aircraft steady. Look at the Altimeter and see that you have gained height due to an increase in lift. Now look at the Airspeed Indicator and notice that there has been a drop in speed. This is due to the increase in drag.

Lowering flap causes an increase in height and loss of airspeed

Therefore to maintain your original height, you will have to lower the nose with the consequence that your forward visibility out of the cockpit is now improved. This is a very useful feature when you are on finals before making a landing.

Alternatively, if want to maintain your height whilst raising your flaps in stages, you can achieve this by raising the nose and re-trimming. You will notice that there is now an increase in airspeed due to the reduction in drag.

We'll next look at using flaps during a descent.

Using Flaps to Steepen Descent

The following exercise will demonstrate how we can use flaps to steepen our descent path. First, imagine setting the aircraft up in straight and level flight. Keep an especial good look out as we will be descending.

Okay, make a final check. Flaps set at zero. Speed will be within the white arc. Do not touch the throttle during this exercise.

Now select the first stage of flap. Maintain your airspeed by lowering the nose of the aircraft.

Lowering flap gives greater forward vision

Continue to select flap in stages until full flap is deployed. Keep you airspeed constant and notice how our flight path is now steeper giving us a much improved view forwards. Finally check your Vertical Speed Indicator (VSI) and note that our rate of descent has increased.

In the final section we will look at how flaps allow us to fly safely with an improved forward vision.

Using Flaps to allow Safe Flight with Improved Forward Vision

This exercise will demonstrate that by deploying flaps, you can safely fly at a lower airspeed and with an improved forward vision.

So imagine you are flying straight and level. Check your Airspeed Indicator and confirm that it is within the white arc for safe flap deployment.

Now, lower the flap in stages and re-trim until you have full flap deployed. Use your elevators to maintain airspeed and power to maintain height.

Next reduce the airspeed to just less than the clean stalling speed for your particular aircraft. You can attain this by bringing the needle to just below the Green Arc on the Airspeed Indicator.

Note that the aircraft can now safely fly at this very much reduced airspeed. Notice that your forward vision is also much improved.

Flaps produce more drag and greater fuel consumption

Finally, a word of warning; flying an aircraft in this configuration will increase your fuel consumption due to the increase in drag. Therefore keep checking your fuel contents, remembering also that they are not reliable indicators, so come down on the side of caution.

Chapter 5

Carburettor Heat Control

Introduction

The carburettor heat control is used to direct hot air into the carburettor in order to prevent or melt away any ice that may have formed in the system.

Selecting carburettor heat should always form part of your en-route FREDA checks (more about FREDA checks in a later section).

However, remember not to select carburettor heat whilst on the ground taxiing the aircraft. This is because the hot air selected is not filtered and therefore could introduce dirt and dust into the carburettor system.

Let's now consider the different conditions of flight when carburettor heat should be selected.

If Ice is Suspected

It is important for a pilot to be able to recognise the signs that ice may be present in the carburettor system. Symptoms of possible carburettor icing include a rough running engine and a drop in engine rpm.

So if you suspect you may have icing, then immediately select Full Carburettor Heat. This is usually achieved by pulling the control knob fully out.

Note that there will be a drop in engine rpm. This is due to the less dense hot air being inducted into the engine cylinders.

If you notice that there is a slight rise in rpm, it could indicate there was some ice present but that it has now melted.

After a short period of time has elapsed or if the engine is running more smoothly, set the carburettor heat control back to Full Cold. You will notice that there will be a rise in engine rpm.

Using Carburettor Heat as a Precaution

Carburettor heat is selected as part of your standard FREDA checks which is carried out at regular intervals throughout a flight.

It is also used when reducing the throttle to idle. Select carburettor heat to Full Hot and then close the throttle.

When you are about to increase power, select carburettor heat to Full Cold first before opening the throttle to the required setting.

In the next section, we will look at the functions of the Mixture Control.

Chapter 6

The Mixture Control

Introduction

The Mixture control has 2 functions;-

to "lean" the fuel/air mixture in order to obtain optimal fuel usage and

to "cut-off" the fuel to the carburettor in order to stop the engine.

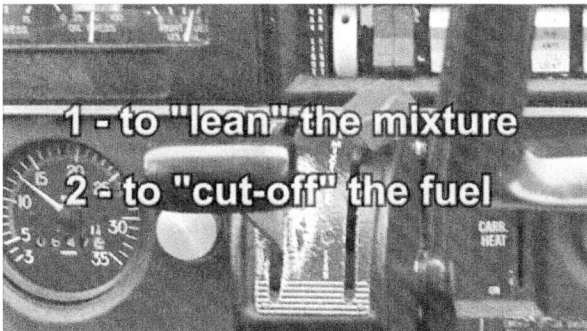

The mixture control has two functions

Let's now consider the occasions when we need to use the mixture control.

To Lean the Mixture at Altitude

It is usual to lean the mixture as you gain altitude. However, you must consult your Pilot's Operating Handbook or ask your Instructor as to what are the recommended values for your particular aircraft. Once you have ascertained this information, you are ready to fly the following exercise.

First, adjust your throttle to set your desired engine rpm.

Then slowly begin to move the red Mixture Control Knob out towards the Lean position. Some aircraft will have a different mixture control, but they will be marked Rich and Lean.

The rpm will rise. If it doesn't, return the Mixture to Rich.

Continue moving the Mixture Control out until a slight drop in rpm occurs.

At this point, move the control Knob back in a short way to restore maximum rpm. It is safer always to be slightly richer than leaner.

If the aircraft is "leaned" correctly, your engine will run better and you will be using fuel more efficiently.

On Descent

This is short but important.

Before commencing a descent and reducing your power setting, select the Mixture Control to Full Rich.

After Landing

Once you have landed and taxied to your parking area, you will go through your Shutdown Checklist. This will obviously entail stopping the engine. Once again, always check for any differences for your particular aircraft.

To stop the engine;-

close the throttle and

move the Mixture Control to Idle Cut-Off by pulling it fully out.

When the engine has stopped, you should continue with any other actions as per your Pilot's Operating Handbook.

Chapter 7

The Radio

Introduction

The use of the radio is a big subject in itself. There is also a theory course on the subject which you will be examined on when you take your Private Pilot's course. There is another guide in this series which covers the radio in a great deal of detail. It is called "The Flight Pilot's Radio Manual." But here, we are just going to consider the basics of how to operate the equipment. You will learn the correct technique and the different types of messages to transmit as part of your normal flying course.

Most training aircraft will have a radio fitted. Some also contain a navigational unit and these are known as a NAV/COM.

Typical NAV/COM unit

Your particular radio unit will be explained by your Instructor, but in general terms, first make sure that your headset or microphone is connected.

Next, switch the unit on and select the desired frequency. Adjust the volume control to a comfortable level.

You may hear unwanted background noise or hiss. By turning the Squelch control you should be able to eliminate it or at least improve the reception of the received signal.

Transmitting a Message

To transmit, hold down the Transmit Button and deliver your message.

When you have finished, release the transmit button and await a reply. Remember that when the transmit button is depressed, no one else can use that frequency.

Finally, in this short introduction to the Radio Unit, do not "double click" the transmit button as this can cause damage to the relay.

Cabin Heating & Ventilation

A modern training aircraft can deliver both warm and cool air to the cabin and there are separate controls for each.

Cabin heating & ventilation controls

But be careful, the warm air is usually tapped off from the engine exhaust system. So if a problem should develop, there is a chance of toxic fumes being introduced into the cabin. Therefore, always select cool air as well as warm air and ensure there is ventilation by opening one of the fresh air vents fitted.

Chapter 8

Taxiing

A full account of the rules concerning taxiing can be found in any good Air Law publication. But there are a number of practical points which are covered here.

When you are about to move off, release the parking brake and apply sufficient power to get the aircraft moving. Next, close the throttle and test the toe brakes. Do this on each side if necessary.

Always taxi at a speed appropriate to conditions

Taxi at a speed appropriate to conditions but this should not exceed a fast walking pace. Do not use Power and Brakes at the same time.

If you have to cross from one surface to another and especially if there is a ridge, try to do so at an angle of 45 degrees and remember to reduce speed.

Whilst taxiing, become aware from which direction the wind is coming from and its strength.

Cross between different surfaces at 45 degrees if possible

In a strong headwind, hold the control column in either the neutral position or slightly back - this has the effect of holding the tail down and takes pressure off the nose-wheel.

With a strong tailwind, hold the control column slightly forward to avoid the tail from lifting.

A strong crosswind from ahead will try to turn the aircraft into wind. Use the rudder to compensate. If the into wind wing tries to lift, turn the control column towards that wing to hold it down.

A strong crosswind from behind can be compensated for by moving the control column away from the wind side. This lowers the wind-side aileron and keeps the wing down.

Remember, as the pilot, you are in charge of keeping the aircraft safe whilst taxiing.

Always be fully aware when taxiing

Chapter 9

Straight & Level Flight

Introduction

There are four main forces acting on an aircraft in flight. They are the aircraft's weight, which acts downwards, the lift which is generated by the wings, the forward motion called thrust and drag which acts in the opposite direction to thrust.

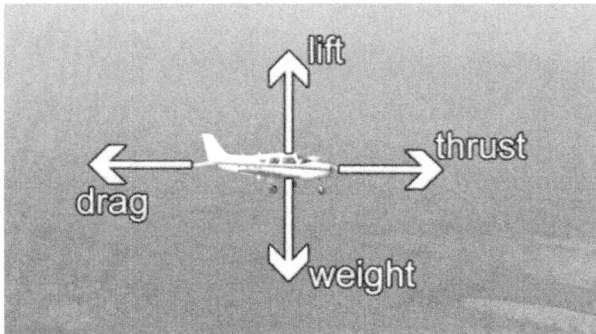

Four main forces acting on an aircraft in flight

If forces are out of balance you need to intervene using flying controls

In steady straight and level flight, lift balances weight and thrust balances drag; the aircraft is said to be in equilibrium.

If all forces are out of equilibrium, input from the control column to the elevators can bring the aircraft back into a state of balance.

Flying Straight and Level at Constant Power

In this section we're going to look at flying the aircraft straight and level and with a constant power setting. Take a good look out.

Then select a reference point on the horizon in order for us to fly straight. Now with cruise power set, use the elevators to place the nose in the cruise attitude.

Select a reference point on the horizon

Check the altimeter and vertical speed indicator; make any small adjustments using the elevators.

Let the airspeed settle. Then perform a cross-check using the altimeter, vertical speed indicator and airspeed indicator. If they are steady, hold the pitch attitude and trim off any excess pressure.

If the aircraft starts to climb, use the elevator to regain your desired height. Hold the nose slightly lower than it was before.

Let the airspeed settle; check the altimeter and vertical speed indicator. When steady, trim off any excess elevator pressure.

On the other hand, if the aircraft starts to descend, use the elevators to regain the desired height. You may have to apply extra power.

Hold the nose slightly higher than before and allow the airspeed to settle.

Cross-check the altimeter and vertical speed indicator and trim off any excess elevator pressure.

If you find the aircraft begins to change heading, use the ailerons to bring it back on heading and the rudder to keep in balance. Maintain height with the elevators.

Flying Straight and Level at a Selected Airspeed

In this exercise we're going to look at flying straight and level at a selected airspeed. First set the aircraft up straight and level and in trim.

We are now going to increase speed in level flight.

Open the throttle to a higher power setting and balance with rudder. Lower the nose to maintain height as the airspeed increases.

Open the throttle to increase speed in straight & level flight

When at the desired airspeed, re-adjust the power setting and trim in the nose-down direction. Continue to make small adjustments using power, attitude and trim as necessary.

We're now going to decrease speed in level flight. Close the throttle and balance with the rudder.

This time, raise the nose to maintain height as the airspeed decays.

When at the selected airspeed, adjust the power setting and trim off any excess elevator pressure. Continue to make small changes to power, attitude and trim as necessary.

To decrease speed in straight & level flight first close throttle & raise the nose

Flying Straight and Level with Flap Extended

We're now going to demonstrate how to fly the aircraft with flaps extended. The advantage of this is that we can fly the aircraft slower and increase our forward vision.

So, first reduce the power until the airspeed indicator is within the white arc. Fly the plane straight and level and trim.

Next, extend the flap in stages. To maintain height and to avoid ballooning the aircraft, push the control column forwards to compensate.

Because of the extra drag you will also have to increase power in order to maintain your desired airspeed.

Remember to trim off excess elevator pressure after each stage of flap has been deployed.

When you are ready to raise the flap, check first that your airspeed is not too low.

Now, raise the flap in stages, this time holding the nose slightly higher to maintain height and to avoid the "sink" associated with raising flap.

Adjust your power setting accordingly and remember to trim off any excess elevator pressure.

Raising flap from full flap can be encountered if you are making a go-around on final.

Chapter 10

Climbing

Each aircraft will have several climb speeds in order to satisfy various criteria. The choice is governed by what the pilot wishes to achieve.

If there are obstacles, a steep angle of climb may be selected and this speed is known as Vx.

The best-rate climb is the speed which allows the aircraft to gain height in as short a time as possible and is termed Vy.

Finally, there is the cruise-climb which is a best compromise between speed and altitude and is the most commonly chosen.

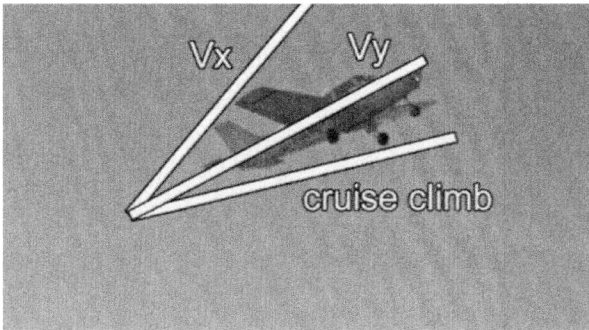

There are three climb speeds published for each aircraft type

Refer to your Pilot's Operating Handbook for the relevant speeds for your particular aircraft.

In this exercise we're going to enter a steady climb, maintain it on a constant heading and then level out at our chosen altitude.

First, trim the aircraft in straight and level flight and keep a good look out above, below and ahead.

Choose a reference point ahead and slightly to the left of the nose in order to still be able to see it when in the climb attitude.

Now, check that the mixture is rich, and open the throttle to climb power, which in most training aircraft is full power. Balance with rudder.

Then raise the nose and let the airspeed settle at the desired speed. Adjust the attitude to maintain this speed.

Trim off any excess elevator pressure. You are now in a steady climb. For safety reasons, make clearing turns every 500 feet or so in order to avoid any other traffic.

Monitor the airspeed, altimeter and vertical speed indicator for sensible readings.

To level off, gradually push the control column forwards to lower the nose until you are at your desired height.

Then allow the airspeed to increase to cruise speed and when there, reduce the power to the cruise setting.

Balance the aircraft and trim off any excess elevator pressure.

Chapter 11

Descending

There are two methods of descending;-

the powered descent and

the unpowered descent, also known as the glide.

We will look at the glide first.

In a glide, you are looking to either stay in the air for as long as possible, known as endurance or you are looking to travel as far as possible which is known as best-range.

There are two types of descent; powered & unpowered

The maximum gliding range is achieved at the speed which also gives the best Lift/Drag ratio. Check this speed in your Pilot's Operating Handbook.

Be aware that a headwind will lower the glide range and a tailwind will extend it.

The best endurance speed is the minimum descent speed as shown on the vertical speed indicator. Typically this is about 25% lower than the best-range speed. But check your Pilot's Operating Handbook for your particular aircraft.

Let's now look at an example.

We're currently flying straight and level, in trim and we want to enter and maintain a steady glide on a constant heading and then to level off at a selected altitude.

First, decide on a glide speed and then choose a reference point ahead. Keep a good look out at all times.

Ok, mixture is rich and carburettor heat is set to full hot. Close the throttle. Balance with rudder and allow the airspeed to decay to your chosen glide speed.

Now, lower the nose to maintain glide speed and trim. Note the attitude.

Control your airspeed using the elevators

As you descend, keep the wings level with ailerons, control the airspeed with elevators and balance using the rudder.

Keep a good look out and make clearing turns every 500 feet or so. Warm the engine periodically by opening the throttle for a few seconds and then close it again.

Monitor the airspeed, altimeter and vertical speed indicator.

To level off, first anticipate your desired height. Open the throttle to cruise power and set the carburettor heat to cold.

Keep the aircraft in balance with the rudder. As you approach cruise speed, raise the nose to straight and level attitude and re-trim.

The Powered Descent

In this powered descent, we will keep the airspeed constant with attitude and use power to maintain it.

The usual powered descent is called the cruise descent and it is entered by reducing the power slightly and lowering the nose attitude to maintain the same speed as in the cruise.

Your aiming point on the ground should remain constant out of the windscreen.

Your aiming point should remain constant out of the window

If the descent rate is too high, open the throttle and adjust the nose attitude a little higher to maintain the desired airspeed. Use the rudder to balance the aircraft and trim.

If the descent rate is too high, open the throttle and adjust the nose attitude a little higher to maintain the desired airspeed. Use the rudder to balance the aircraft and trim.

Use of Flap in the Descent

Flaps are used in the descent in order to steepen it.

Before extending flaps, make sure the airspeed is within the white arc.

Now, lower the flap in stages. To maintain the airspeed, adjust the nose to a lower attitude. Remember to trim off any excess elevator pressure.

The Sideslip

By using "crossed controls", in other words, using the ailerons against the rudder will lead to an increased rate of descent without the need for flap.

Make sure that this exercise is permitted in your particular aircraft. Check your Pilot's Operating Handbook or check with your Instructor first.

Ok, we're in a normal steady descent. First, apply bank with ailerons and maintain the heading by using opposite rudder.

In other words, if you move the control column to the right, then apply left rudder in order to hold the heading.

Apply bank & opposite rudder input

Keep the nose attitude steady and make any necessary adjustments with elevators to maintain airspeed.

The greater the amount of bank you put on, the more opposite rudder you have to use to maintain heading and the steeper the rate of descent.

The greater the amount of bank you put on, the more opposite rudder you have to use to maintain heading and the steeper the rate of descent.

Maintain airspeed with elevators.

Chapter 12

Turning

The Medium Level Turn

The medium level turn is one that is flown at a constant height, at an angle of bank not exceeding 30 degrees, a steady power setting and the aircraft in balance.

With the aircraft flying straight and level and in trim, maintain a good look out and select a reference point for roll out.

Move the control column to the left and the aircraft banks in the same direction. When the correct amount of bank is achieved, centre the column and balance with rudder. Maintain height by easing back the control column and raising the nose attitude.

When bank angle is achieved, centre the control column

If the aircraft gains height, either increase the bank angle or ease off the back pressure on the control column.

If the aircraft starts to lose height, either decrease the angle of bank or raise the nose.

Before rolling out, anticipate the reference point. Then level the wings with the ailerons, balance the aircraft with rudder and ease the back pressure on the control column.

The Climbing Turn

During the climbing turn, we'll demonstrate that the rate of climb will decrease compared to the straight climb.

Ok imagine the aircraft is in a steady climb at full power. Select a reference point for roll out.

Now use the ailerons to roll the aircraft into a bank angle not exceeding 20 degrees. Balance with rudder and lower the nose to maintain airspeed.

Do not exceed 20 degrees bank angle

Before roll out, anticipate the reference point and level the wings. Balance the aircraft with rudder and use the elevators to lower the nose in order to maintain the desired airspeed.

Descending Turns

There are four types of descending turns;

the gliding turn,

the descending turn using power,

the descending turn using flaps and

the sideslip whilst in a descending turn.

The Gliding Turn

There are two points to remember in a gliding turn

first the airspeed decreases so you have to lower the nose and

second the rate of descent increases.

So when you come to practice this exercise, first establish the aircraft in a steady glide. Decide on a reference point to roll out on and keep a good look out.

Roll the aircraft into a bank not exceeding 30 degrees. Balance with rudder input and lower the nose to maintain descent speed.

Anticipate your roll out reference point

Anticipate the reference point and roll the wings level, re-balance with the rudder pedals and raise the nose to maintain the desired descent speed.

The Descending Turn Using Power

First, establish the aircraft in a powered descent with the airspeed and rate of descent constant. As always, keep a good look out.

First, establish the aircraft in a powered descent with the airspeed and rate of descent constant. As always, keep a good look out.

Because airspeed decreases in a turn, add more power with the throttle. Remember, the steeper the turn, the more power required.

High descent rate – add power & raise nose

If the rate of descent is too high, add power and raise the nose to maintain the desired airspeed.

Low descent rate – reduce power & lower nose

If the rate of descent is too low, reduce the power and lower the nose slightly to maintain airspeed.

To roll out of the manoeuvre, anticipate the chosen reference point, level the wings, balance with rudder and reduce power to maintain the desired rate of descent. Remember, the airspeed is controlled by use of the elevators.

Descending Turns with Flap Extended

One of the points to remember when flying with flaps extended is that a lower nose attitude is needed to maintain the same airspeed.

In this example, the aircraft is descending with 2 stages of flap deployed. This is a configuration quite often encountered before turning onto finals for landing.

Now, roll the aircraft into a bank angle not exceeding 30 degrees. Balance with rudder. Notice that a lower nose attitude is required to maintain the desired airspeed.

Also note that forward visibility has been improved by the lower nose attitude which is an advantage in coming in to land.

Do not exceed 30 degrees bank angle

Sideslipping in a Descending Turn

Applying ailerons against rudder, in other words, crossing the controls, results in a rapid loss of height and is known as sideslipping.

You must check that your aircraft is permitted this manoeuvre by referring to the Pilot's Operating Handbook or by asking your instructor.

Ok imagine we're established in a steady gliding turn with the correct amount of aileron set.

Now, apply opposite rudder; in other words, if you're banked to the left, apply right rudder.

Move the control column forward in order to lower the nose and maintain airspeed.

Note that the rate of descent has increased.

To stop the sideslip, centre the balance ball with the rudder and control the bank angle with the ailerons.

Remember that during a sideslip, airspeed is controlled by elevators and the rate of descent by the bank angle and the out of balance rudder input.

Turning onto Selected Headings

There are three ways to turn onto a selected magnetic heading;

by using the Direction Indicator,

using the Turn Co-ordinator and finally

using the Magnetic Compass.

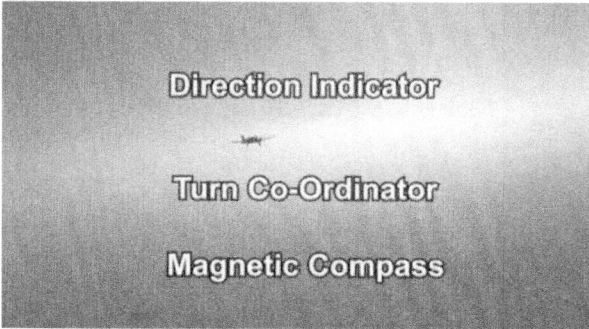

Three methods of turning onto selected magnetic headings

Using the Direction Indicator

To turn onto a selected heading using the direction indicator, first fly straight and level, in balance and check that the DI is in agreement with the magnetic compass. This action also forms part of your en-route FREDA checks.

Check the DI & compass are in agreement

Decide whether you are going to turn left or right and make a good look out.

Proceed with a normal turn and check the DI periodically.

Anticipate the roll out by about 5 degrees or so by smoothly levelling the wings and balancing with rudder.

Using the Turn Co-Ordinator and Clock

An alternative way to turn onto a selected heading is to use the turn co-ordinator and clock. If a turn is conducted at Rate 1 as marked on the turn co-ordinator dial, the aircraft will change heading at a rate of 3 degrees per second or 90 degrees every 30 seconds.

For example, if we want to turn right from a present heading of 060 degrees magnetic to a new heading of 180 degrees, the heading change is 120 degrees.

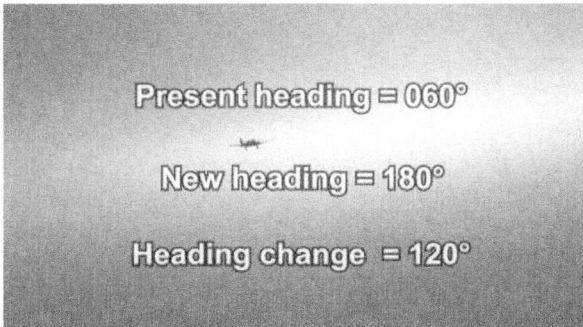

Present heading = 060°

New heading = 180°

Heading change = 120°

Work out the change in heading

Heading Change

$$\frac{120°}{3} = 40 \text{ seconds}$$

Divide heading change by the rate of change to give the turning time

If we divide this number by our rate of change which is 3 degrees per second, we can see that it will take 40 seconds to make the heading change.

Using the Magnetic Compass

The final method, the magnetic compass, is not recommended as a first choice because of inherent inaccuracies. But, if using the compass, there are a number of points to remember.

The magnetic compass has some inherent inaccuracies

When turning onto a Northerly heading, you should roll out approximately 30 degrees before the desired heading.

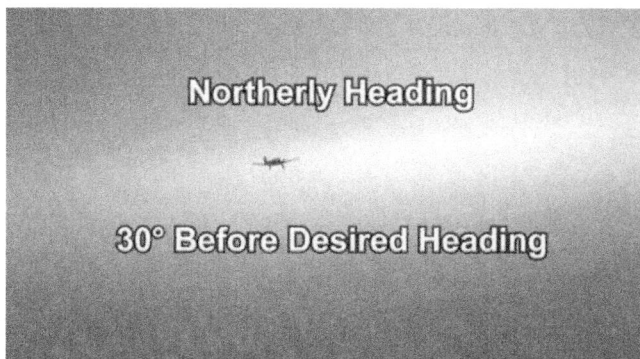

Northerly heading – roll out early

If turning onto a Southerly heading, you should aim to roll out approximately 30 degrees past the desired new heading.

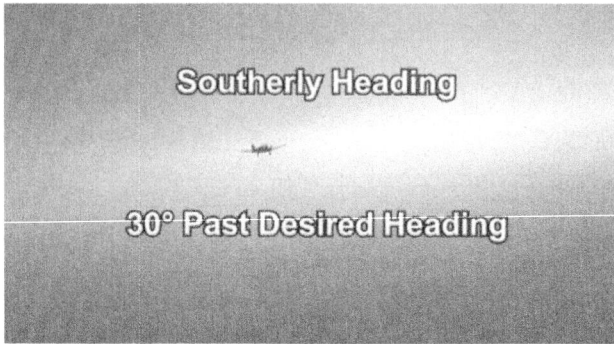

Southerly heading – roll out later

If you are turning onto an Easterly or Westerly heading, little or no allowance is necessary.

East/west headings – little change

If your angle of bank is less than 30 degrees, you can also reduce the above allowances.

Remember, use the DI method first and leave the compass as a third option.

Chapter 13

Stalling

Stalling occurs when the airflow over the wing breaks down due to the critical angle of attack being exceeded. Be aware, stalling can occur when the aircraft is in any configuration and, more importantly, at any speed. Exceeding the critical angle of attack is what causes stalling.

The basic stalling speed for a particular aircraft is known as Vs1 and is indicated on the airspeed indicator as the lower end of the green arc. This figure assumes the aircraft is at maximum weight, the wings are level and no flaps extended.

Vs1 is lower end of the green arc

The stall speed with full flap extended is known as Vs0 and is shown on the ASI as the lower end of the white arc. Refer to your Pilot's Operating Handbook for your particular figures.

Let's now proceed through a typical exercise in stalling practice.

Stall Recovery Using Power

We're flying straight and level and the aircraft is in trim.

But, before we begin, we must do a HASELL check.

Make your HASELL check before beginning exercise

H – is there sufficient height for us to recover by 3000 feet?

A – stands for airframe; are we in trim, are the flaps in the desired position? Yes, in this case they're clean.

S – is for security, are hatches and harnesses secure and are there any loose objects?

E – is for engine. Check T and Ps are in the green, fuel contents checked and mixture and carb heat as required?

L – the first L stands for location. Make sure we are not above any town or village.

L – the final L is for look out. Make sure the area around is clear of other traffic.

Having completed our HASELL check, select carb heat to hot, then close the throttle and maintain height by easing back on the control column.

Keep the ailerons neutral and instead use the rudder to keep the aircraft straight and the wings level.

As we approach the stall speed, note that the airspeed is decreasing and the controls are feeling less firm.

The pre-stall warning horn will sound and you will start to feel a shudder in the control column. By now, the nose of the aircraft is high.

As the aircraft stalls, the nose drops and the aircraft sinks.

To recover, simultaneously lower the nose with the control column and apply full power with the throttle. Set carb heat to cold. Use rudder input to control engine torque.

As the airspeed increases, ease the nose up to straight and level flight and adjust the controls to your desired setting.

Check the altimeter; you should only have lost about 50 feet.

Stall Recovery Without Using Power

To recover from a stall without using power, once again go through the HASELL checks and as before, bring the aircraft up to the point of stall.

This time, as it stalls, release back pressure on the control column and positively lower the nose. The attitude selected will be lower than the stall recovery with power.

Allow the airspeed to recover, and ease back the control column to level flight. Add power to gain your desired flight configuration.

This time, the height loss will be more, in the region of 200 feet.

Once again, remember that stalling can occur in any configuration; climbing, descending, turning and with or without flaps. So take the time to practice each with your instructor.

Chapter 14

Slow Flight

Flying an aircraft at minimum power means that its fuel consumption is also at a minimum. Therefore it's operating at its maximum endurance and the airspeed associated with this is called the endurance speed.

Any speed less than an aircraft's endurance speed is termed as slow flight and is characterised by having to apply more power as speed decreases. This is due to the high angle of attack necessary and the consequent increase in drag.

Let's look at slow flight. Reduce power and raise the nose to maintain height. The slow airspeed you choose to fly at should be discussed with your instructor first.

When the desired airspeed is reached, increase power and continually adjust throttle and attitude to maintain the airspeed.

Use throttle & attitude to maintain slow airspeed

If the airspeed increases, raise the nose and reduce power.

If the airspeed decreases, lower the nose and add power.

The co-ordination of elevator, throttle and rudder are crucial when flying at slow speeds.

Chapter 15

Spinning

A spin occurs when a stalled aircraft enters a spiral descent. It is in motion about all three axes.

In a spin, the aircraft is simultaneously, stalled, rolling, pitching, yawing and sideslipping. And on top of that, it is rapidly losing height.

The flight instruments would read, low airspeed, altimeter decreasing rapidly, VSI reading a high rate of descent, the turn co-ordinator steeply banked and the balance ball out to the side. Both the attitude and direction indicators would have toppled and be useless.

You may even be unsure of the direction of spin. So use the turn co-ordinator as a reference. A look out can also confirm the direction of spin.

Full Spins

Before attempting this exercise, make sure that your particular aircraft is permitted full spins.

Remember to carry out the HASELL check. Then select carb heat to full hot and close the throttle. Ease back on the control column in order to maintain height. Keep the wings level by using input from the rudder.

When the aircraft is about to stall, smoothly apply full rudder in the direction in which you wish to spin. Hold the control column fully back.

Whilst in the developed spin, keep the control column fully back, keep the rudder hard over and hold the ailerons neutral.

To recover, make sure the throttle is closed and the ailerons are still neutral. Confirm the direction of spin by checking the turn co-ordinator.

Next, apply full opposite rudder. Wait a moment and ease the control column forward in order to unstall the wings. Maintain until the rotation stops.

Then centralise the rudder and level the wings. The aircraft is now in a dive. Ease back on the control column until in level flight.

As you reach straight and level attitude, add sufficient power to continue the flight and set the carb heat to cold.

At this point, you should still be at a height of at least 3000 feet.

Incipient Spins

This exercise allows us to recognise the onset of a spin and to stop it before it develops.

Ok, the aircraft is approaching the stall. Apply full rudder in the desired direction of spin.

As the spin starts, simultaneously ease the control column forwards to unstall the wings, apply sufficient rudder to prevent further yaw and open the throttle to maximum.

The airspeed increases and the wings become unstalled. Now, level the wings with ailerons and rudder and ease out of the descent. Resume your normal flight.

In this example, note that the loss of height is much less.

Chapter 16

Standard Take-Off

&

Climb to Downwind Leg

Before any flight, there are a number of checklists to follow as explained earlier in this book. But remember, only use the authorised checklist found in your Pilot's Operating Handbook or the one used by your authorised flight training organisation.

Pre-planning is essential before every flight

A standard circuit consists of four legs and all turns are to the left unless specified. As a general guide, climb to at least 500 feet above aerodrome level before turning left onto the crosswind leg.

Continue to circuit height, usually about 1000 feet and then turn left onto the downwind leg, parallel to the runway. Pre-landing checks and a radio call are made on this leg.

Turn left onto base leg and start descent to about 500 feet before turning finals for landing.

Finals to land

Be careful to check the procedures for your particular airfield first.

Ok let's now take a look at a typical take-off and initial climb to the downwind leg.

So we will join our flight at the stage when we have made all our checks including power and pre-take-off and we're at the holding point of the active runway.

Before lining up, check carefully that the runway and approach are clear of other traffic. When clear, line up.

Make sure you are on the centre line and that the nose wheel is straight. Select a reference point in the distance. Check wind direction.

Check the DI corresponds with the compass and the orientation of the runway. Next brakes off, put your heels on the floor and open the throttle to 2000 rpm before applying full power.

Use appropriate rudder input to keep the aircraft on the centre line and check the engine gauge to confirm the correct rpm.

As the speed increases, check the ASI is working.

Check your ASI during the take-off roll

Start to ease back on the control column and at take-off speed, lift off and gradually assume the climb attitude. Keep the wings level with ailerons, balance with rudder and maintain climb attitude with elevators.

At about 300 feet, raise any take-off flap, using attitude to avoid any "sink". Trim the aircraft.

At about 500 feet, start a climbing turn to the left onto the crosswind leg. Keep the bank angle to 20 degrees or less and maintain climb speed using the elevators.

Select a new reference point. Allow for drift and climb to circuit height.

We're at 1000 feet above aerodrome level, so look carefully around for any conflicting traffic and when clear, make a medium turn left taking us onto the downwind leg.

Once established, make a downwind radio call.

At this moment, let's break away from the flight and look at two emergency drills associated with take-offs; the engine failure after take-off and the discontinued take-off.

Make medium turns within the circuit

Engine Failure After Take-Off

The engine failure after take-off is one where time is of the essence, so you need to have a clear plan of action. We've applied full power and are approaching take-off. Please note that as this exercise takes place close to the ground, it should only be practiced with your instructor.

The first priority is to maintain flying speed. Do not be tempted to try to turn back to the airfield; if you're low, you won't make it.

Ok, the aircraft is in a steady climb, passing through 500 feet and there is no flap deployed.

To simulate an engine failure, select carb heat to hot and smoothly close the throttle.

Immediately lower the nose to maintain flying speed. Look ahead for a suitable landing field that is within range. The field should ideally be within 30 degrees of the nose and limit any turns to 15 degrees of bank or less. You should try to land into wind if possible.

Immediately lower the nose & locate a suitable landing field

You may not have time to carry out any engine checks or make a radio call. When you are committed to landing, turn the fuel and ignition off and any other actions detailed in the Pilot's Operating Handbook.

Use flap as necessary.

After landing, if possible, shutdown and secure the aircraft.

Discontinued Take-Off

There are a number of reasons why a take-off may have to be aborted. There could be an obstacle on the runway or you may experience problems with the engine or instruments such as the ASI not working.

As soon as you decide to abort, close the throttle, keep the aircraft straight using rudder input and apply the brakes firmly.

Position the aircraft off the runway if possible

Before stopping, try to position the aircraft off the runway and notify the ATS unit.

Chapter 17

Circuit Operations,

Approaches & Landings

One of the most crucial areas of flight training is the approach and landing. Experience and the appreciation of the factors involved will lead to the safe conclusion of every flight.

Circuit, Powered Approach and Normal Landing

We're presently on the downwind leg with the aircraft at circuit height and in trim. Start the pre-landing checks as detailed for your particular aircraft.

These may include brakes off, the undercarriage is down unless it is fixed, the mixture is rich, the correct fuel tank selected and the contents sufficient, the fuel pump on and the primer locked. Also check that hatches and harnesses are secure. The downwind radio call can be made.

Downwind in the circuit

When the runway is in your 8 o-clock position, make a medium turn to the left; not exceeding 30 degrees of bank angle.

We're now on base leg. Select carb heat to hot and reduce power. Allow the airspeed to move into the white arc and deploy, in this case, two stages of flap.

Maintain your chosen rate of descent by using power and your airspeed with elevator input. Trim the aircraft.

Anticipate the extended line of the runway and commence a descending turn to the left onto final approach. Your height will normally be no lower than 500 feet and your angle of bank between 15–20 degrees.

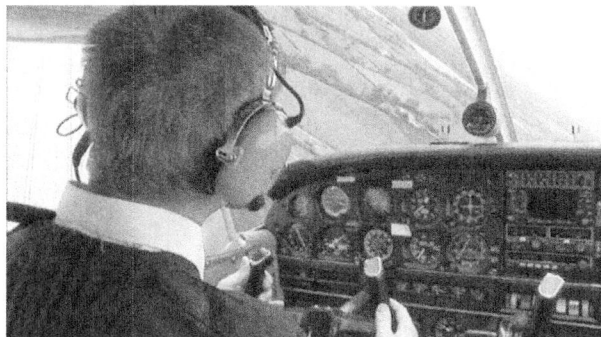

Do not exceed recommended bank angles

Once established on finals, select full flap if it is appropriate.

Hold the attitude to attain final approach speed and then lower the nose to maintain it. Trim the aircraft.

Try to keep your aiming point in a constant position in the windscreen.

Select carb heat to cold and make your finals radio call.

At about 20 feet above the runway, commence the flare and smoothly close the throttle. Raise the nose slightly to reduce the sink rate.

Progressively raise the nose to hold off the aircraft just above the runway.

Lower the nose down gently after main gear

Touchdown on the main undercarriage wheels and hold the nose wheel off for a few seconds until you can gently lower it onto the runway. Keep straight using the rudder pedals.

Apply the brake as necessary to slow the aircraft down.

The Go-Around

There are many reasons you may elect to abandon a landing and go-around for another approach. But when you are faced with this decision, decide positively and perform it decisively.

OK, the aircraft is on finals and full flap has been extended. At this point we find that we cannot land safely and decide to go-around.

Open the throttle to full power and select carb heat to cold. Raise the nose to the appropriate pitch attitude to maintain speed and then trim.

Now raise the flaps in stages and adjust the pitch attitude slightly higher. Maintain airspeed with elevators. Re-trim and continue to climb back to circuit height.

Departing and Joining the Circuit

The correct procedure for departing and joining the circuit depends on the particular airfield concerned. Current information can be obtained by talking to the ATS unit, consulting the relevant CAP Publication or by asking your instructor.

Always obtain current information from ATC or your instructor

As a general guide, follow any ATC instructions. If there isn't a unit available, plan a departure that will not interfere with any other traffic. Examples can include extending the upwind leg or departing the circuit from the downwind leg.

Remember to check your altimeter is set to QNH after departure.

Before joining a circuit, you should be aware of the airfield QNH, elevation and the current QFE if required.

The method of entering a circuit will normally be through ATC instruction.

Alternatively, if no radio service is available, over-fly the airfield at 2000 feet AGL and check the windsock and signals area. Then descend on the dead side and join the downwind leg at circuit height.

Obtain the current QNH/QFE before entering the circuit

The Flapless Approach and Landing

A flapless approach becomes necessary if any part of the flap system fails. Flapless approaches are also advisable if there is a strong gusty wind blowing or if crosswind conditions exist.

The aircraft is now downwind in the circuit and the pre-landing checks have been completed. For a practice approach, you should also have decided on the approach speed to be used.

Extend the downwind leg for a flapless approach

A flapless approach is much flatter, so extend the downwind leg until the runway is in your 7 o-clock position.

Turn onto base leg and select carb heat to hot. Reduce the power earlier than normal.

Control your airspeed carefully on a flapless approach

Commence a descending turn onto finals earlier than on a normal approach. You have to control your airspeed more precisely in a flapless approach.

Remember to select carb heat to cold in case you have to go-around.

Notice that the approach speed is higher due to the higher stalling speed of a clean aircraft. Also note that the forward vision is restricted due to the higher nose attitude we have adopted.

Approach is flatter with no flaps deployed

As we hold the aircraft off, be aware of the extra float due to the decreased drag. In addition, a too high nose attitude may result in the tail scraping the runway.

After landing, apply normal braking, but note the longer landing roll out.

The Glide Approach and Landing

The glide approach is a useful exercise for practicing forced landings after an engine failure. The important point to remember is that on a glide approach, the flight path angle to the runway is controlled by use of the flaps; by extending the flaps you will steepen the descent.

OK, the aircraft is downwind and the pre-landing checks have been completed. Because our range will be decreased in the glide, turn onto base leg earlier than you would normally.

Turn onto base leg earlier when making a glide approach

Wait until the aiming point on the runway is at an angle of about 45 degrees off the nose. Then select carb heat to hot and close the throttle.

Maintain height until the airspeed decays to the glide speed for your particular aircraft. Once it does, adopt the glide attitude necessary to maintain that speed and trim.

Do not extend any flap until you are close to turning onto finals which will be shorter than normal.

The turn onto finals will be shorter than normal

Ok, select the first stage of flap and make a medium turn onto finals. Remember to maintain airspeed in the turn and keep the angle of bank to about 20 degrees.

Once established on finals, select the second stage of flap. Notice that the aircraft is higher than usual with our aiming point about a third of the way up the runway. Only when we are sure of making the runway, do we extend full flap.

Use full flap only when you can definitely make the runway

Because this is a practice, select carb heat to cold in case a go-around becomes necessary.

As the approach angle is steeper, be prepared to execute a more pronounced round-out before landing.

Use brakes as required in order to slow the aircraft down.

If you find you're too high on approach, lower more flap or extend the base leg a little and then turn back onto final approach.

On the other hand, if you find that the aircraft is too low on approach, delay extending any flap or cut in on the turn onto finals.

Crosswind Operations

There may be occasions when you are not able to take-off and land into wind. Every aircraft will have its own crosswind limit and this can be found in your Pilot's Operating Handbook. The other limit to bear in mind is your own limit of competency.

The size of the crosswind component can be estimated as follows;-

30 degrees off the runway heading, then the crosswind component is ½ the wind strength.

30 degree crosswind calculation

45 degrees off the nose gives a crosswind component of 2/3 the wind strength.

45 degree crosswind calculation

60 degrees gives a component of 9/10 the wind strength.

60 degree crosswind calculation

90 degrees and it is all crosswind.

90 degrees – it is all crosswind

Crosswind Take-Off

To demonstrate a crosswind take-off, we are lined up on a suitable runway. So, brakes off, apply full power and move the control column so that the ailerons are into wind.

Keep the aircraft on the centre line using the rudder and hold the nose wheel gently but firmly on the ground.

When the airspeed is slightly higher than the normal take-off speed, ease the control column back and lift off cleanly.

Adopt the climb attitude and at the same time, uncross the controls and turn into wind just enough to allow for drift.

At the normal height, turn onto the crosswind leg and adjust for a change in head or tailwind component. Allow for drift.

Level off at circuit height and turn onto the downwind leg. Again, allow for the new drift. Make your downwind radio call.

Crosswind Landings

There are three accepted techniques to making a crosswind landing. They are called the Crab method, the Wing-Down method and the Combination method.

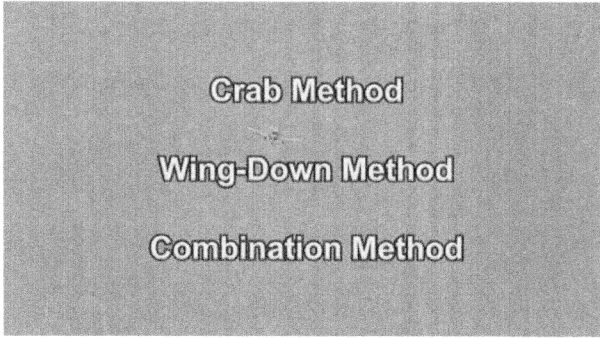

Crosswind landing – the three methods

The Crab Method

We're on final approach for a crosswind landing using the crab method.

Aim the nose into wind in order to keep the aircraft on the extended centre line of the runway.

Aim the nose into wind on approach

As always, control the airspeed with elevators, the flight path with power and the balance with rudder input. Keep the wings level with ailerons except when adjusting the crab angle.

As we begin to flare, come off the power and begin to raise the nose. Maintain the crab into wind.

Maintain crab into wind until just before touchdown

Just before touching down, align the aircraft with the centre line using the rudder and hold the wings level with ailerons.

After touchdown, keep the wheels straight using the rudder and lower the nose wheel onto the runway.

Now move the ailerons into wind in order to keep the aircraft level. Steer with the rudder and apply brakes to slow down.

The Wing-Down Method

We're again on final approach for a crosswind landing; this time using the wing-down method.

Cross the controls by lowering the into wind wing using ailerons and keep on track by employing opposite rudder.

Lower the into wind wing and use opposite rudder to keep on track

Again, control the airspeed with the elevators, the flight path with the power and the track with the combination of wing-down and opposite rudder.

Touchdown on the into wind wheel first

As we begin to flare, reduce power and raise the nose. Maintain track.

We touchdown on the into wind wheel as it is closer to the ground. The other wheel follows naturally.

Keep straight with rudder and lower the nose wheel. Apply into wind aileron to keep the wings level and apply brakes as required.

The Combination Method

The combination method uses the crab method for the approach and the wing-down method for the landing.

So, as we're on final approach, adopt the crab attitude. Notice the alignment of the nose with respect to the runway.

The combination method approach

As we begin to flare at about 20 feet above the runway, use the rudder to align the aircraft with the centre line and lower the into wind wing with aileron input. This prevents any sideways drift.

Now, reduce power and raise the nose. Maintain the centre line using the wing-down aileron and opposite rudder.

Maintain the centre line

Touchdown on the into wind wheel and allow the other wheel to follow naturally. Use the rudder to keep straight.

Then lower the nose wheel onto the runway and use any necessary into wind aileron to keep the wings level. Apply brakes.

Short Field Operations

A short field is defined as one where the runway length available or the obstacle clearance gradient is only just sufficient to satisfy the take-off and landing requirements for your particular aircraft.

These figures can be found in the Performance Charts contained your Pilot's Operating Handbook.

Short Field Take-Off

In general, you should aim to use the shortest ground-run coupled with the steepest climb-out.

To achieve this, consider the following points;-

Take-off into wind,

Use the optimum flap setting,

Make use of as much runway as possible,

Only release brakes when at full power,

Lift-off at the minimum recommended take-off speed,

Use the best angle of climb and

When clear of obstacles, adopt the normal climb attitude.

Short Field Landings

A short field landing can be carried out not only when the landing distance is limited, but also when the landing surface is unknown.

The following considerations should be taken into account when contemplating a short field landing;-

Fly at a slow but safe approach speed,

Keep clear of any possible obstacles,

Do not prolong the hold-off before landing and brake early, but beware of skidding.

Soft Field Operations

A soft field does not have to consist of substances such as sand or snow; it can equally apply to a surface of wet grass or any rough terrain.

Be aware that soft surfaces create extra frictional drag and can put significant additional stress and strain on the undercarriage.

Soft Field Take-Off

With a soft field take-off, you should aim to transfer the weight from the wheels to the wings in as short a time as possible.

Therefore, you should select the optimum flap setting and use full power.

Remember also, to keep the weight off the nose wheel by easing back on the control column. Lift off as soon as it is safe to do so and fly straight and low in order to build up your airspeed before adopting the normal climb attitude.

Soft Field Landing

With soft field landings, the danger comes from the wheels digging into the surface; this is especially so as regarding the nose wheel.

Therefore, aim to land as slowly as safely possible and, after landing, hold the nose wheel off for as long as you can during the landing roll-out. Use full flap if possible.

Chapter 18

First Solo

This is the one exercise you can only do once in your life. From this point on, you can really believe that you're becoming a real pilot.

The exercise itself consists of a normal take-off, circuit and landing at your chosen airfield. Remember to just put into practice all the things you've been taught and experienced with your instructor.

Be confident, because your instructor would not have signed you off if he or she were not confident in your abilities, not only in general handling, but also acting correctly in the unlikely instance of encountering any problems.

Perhaps the most noticeable difference you will find will be in the increased performance of your aircraft; with one less person on board, you can really feel the improvement. So, good luck and enjoy.

Notice the increase in performance due to less weight on board

Chapter 19

Advanced Turning

The Steep Level Turn

A step turn will increase the Load Factor experienced by the pilot and the aircraft.

For example, a banked turn of 60 degrees doubles the load factor making the pilot feel twice as heavy as normal.

To maintain steady flight, lift has to increase to equal the extra load and this is achieved by pulling back on the control column.

However, this also has the effect of increasing the angle of attack and this in turn will increase the speed at which the aircraft stalls. In a 60 degree banked turn, the stall speed increases by 40%.

In addition, there is an increase in induced drag which means more power has to be applied. In essence, this means that the maximum angle of bank in a steady steep turn is determined by the maximum power available.

Very well, let's now take a look at flying a typical steep turn.

Before practicing a steep turn, carry out the HASELL check.

First, select a reference point on the horizon. Then roll the aircraft using ailerons and balance with rudder.

Ease back on the control column to maintain height and start to apply more power. Allow the bank angle to develop to 60 degrees.

Bank angle of 60 degrees

Maintain the bank angle with ailerons and balance with rudder. Height is maintained with elevators and airspeed with power.

If height is gained, reduce the back pressure on the control column and consider steepening the bank angle.

If height is being lost, reduce the bank angle and raise the nose. When steady, re-apply bank.

To roll-out from a steep turn, anticipate your roll-out reference point by about 30 degrees and level the wings with ailerons. Balance with rudder and release the back pressure on the control column to maintain height.

Finally, reduce power to maintain airspeed.

Unusual Attitudes

Unusual attitudes are potentially hazardous and in general, take two forms.

The first is a nose high / steep bank configuration where the decreasing airspeed could lead to a stall or a spin.

The second is a low nose / high speed attitude which, if not corrected, could develop into a spiral dive with the possibility of also exceeding your maximum airspeed, Vne.

Nose High / Low Airspeed

You can recognise this type of attitude primarily from the ASI. It will read low and getting lower.

To recover, simultaneously push the control column forward and roll the wings level. Then add power to bring the airspeed back to the correct setting.

Nose high/low airspeed

A word of warning, if the aircraft appears to be close to a stall, do not use the ailerons to roll the wings level until the wings have become safely unstalled.

Nose Low / High Airspeed

The nose low / high airspeed attitude is recognised primarily from the Airspeed Indicator and Vertical Speed Indicator.

To recover, reduce power and roll the wings level with ailerons. Then use rudder to balance the aircraft.

Nose low/high airspeed

Ease out of the dive using elevators and add power as the nose of the aircraft passes the horizon.

Steep Descending Turns

A steep descending turn can be made in a glide or with power applied.

Because the stalling speed of an aircraft increases in a turn, you should aim to fly at a higher airspeed than normal. Remember that the airspeed is maintained by using the elevators.

Before commencing this manoeuvre, run through your HASELL check.

First, select a reference point on the horizon. Then bank the aircraft to the desired angle using ailerons and balance with rudder.

Hold the nose slightly lower in order to maintain the increased airspeed.

The bank angle is held using ailerons and the balance through rudder input.

Bank angle held using ailerons and rudder to balance

If you notice the airspeed becoming too high, reduce the angle of bank and raise the nose. When the airspeed reaches the desired setting, you can re-apply bank.

To roll out, level the wings using the ailerons use rudder to balance and select the desired pitch with elevators.

Finally, adjust power to the required setting.

Chapter 20

The Forced Landing

Without Using Power

An engine suddenly cutting out may be imagined as a pilot's worst nightmare. But this is a rare event. The main causes are fuel starvation, magneto problems, a mechanical failure or possibly from a birdstrike.

Whatever the cause you as the pilot, will have been trained to cope safely with the situation.

Most modern training aircraft have good gliding characteristics and with a reasonably slow landing speed, can get safely into even quite small fields.

The golden rule to remember is to keep flying the aircraft; and you do that primarily by scanning your airspeed.

If you are an experienced pilot and time allows, you might try to restart the engine. If not, or if time is short, fly the aircraft and follow the forced landing procedure.

There are a couple of accepted ways to execute a forced landing without the use of power.

One of the commonest techniques of carrying out a forced landing without power is called the High Key/Low Key method. Currently, we're at 3000 feet in a suitable area for demonstrating this exercise. Remember to keep a good look out at all times.

To simulate an engine failure, select Carb Heat to Hot, close the throttle and move the Mixture to rich.

The high key/low key method can be used for a forced landing

Convert any excess speed to gain some additional height and put the aircraft into a glide attitude.

If there is no wind component, a light aircraft at 2000 feet should have a gliding range of 3 nautical miles.

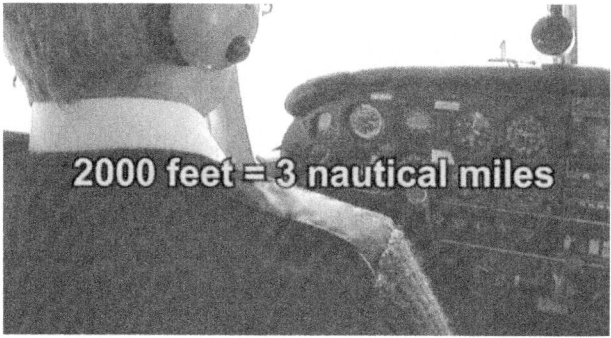

At 2,000 feet – gliding range is 3 nautical miles

Be aware that a headwind will shorten this distance and a tailwind will extend it.

headwind shortens range

tailwind extends range

Be aware of any headwind component

If time allows, make a practice Emergency Check in order to try to restart the engine. If applicable, this will include changing fuel tanks, checking the mixture, the primer and magnetos. There will be a list for your particular aircraft and you should have memorised it.

Now with the aircraft in trim, look for a suitable field or landing area. Take into consideration the following five "Ss".

Size, is it large enough?

Shape, is it long and into wind?

Surface, is it firm with no obstacles including power cables?

Slope, is it level or uphill? We don't want a down-slope if we can help it.

Finally, Surroundings, is it clear of obstacles on approach and is it close to habitation where help can be sought?

Once you have selected a suitable area, try to keep it in sight at all times.

We can now plan our approach and select our Key positions.

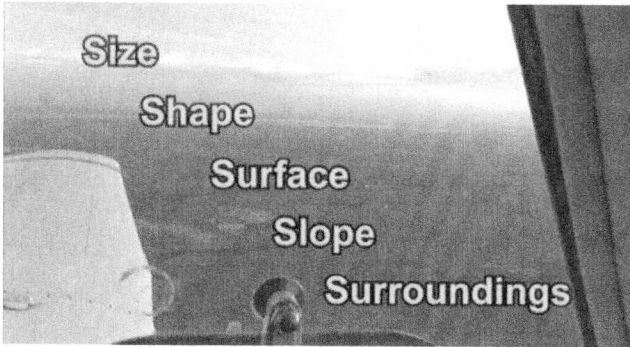

Criteria for a suitable landing field

The High Key point is about 2500 feet above ground and positioned approximately one nautical mile upwind of and in line with, the far end of the landing strip.

The Low Key point is at about 1500 feet above the ground and is positioned approximately ½ a nautical mile abeam the landing threshold.

Because the throttle is closed and this is a practice, remember to warm the engine every so often by opening the throttle for a couple of seconds.

We are now at the High Key point and we look out to verify this.

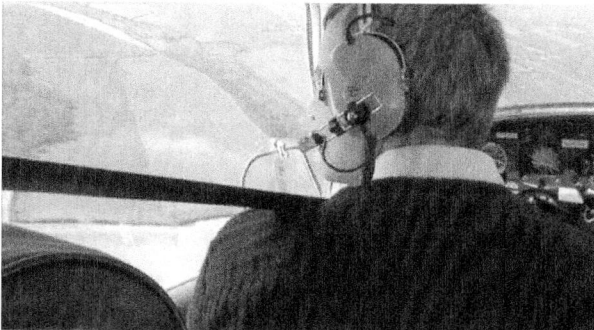

Confirm you are at the High Key

During the whole descent, remember to monitor your instruments especially the airspeed.

At this point, if time allows, make a Simulated Mayday Call.

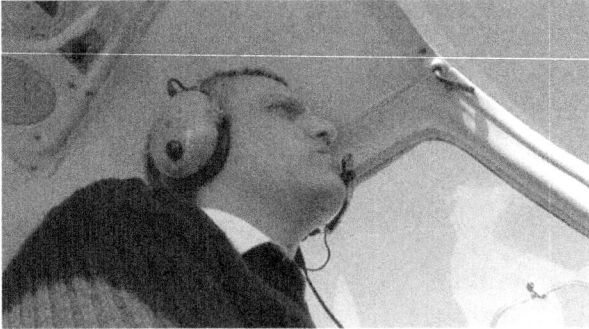

If an exercise, make a simulated Mayday call

You should also simulate switching the Transponder to squawk 7700.

Ok, we're approaching our Low Key point; check the height is about 1500 feet AGL and we are abeam the landing point at about ½ a nautical mile distance. Taking the wind into account, turn onto base leg. Select a stage of flap if you feel confident of reaching your landing point. Remember, flap will steepen your descent.

You are committed to a landing, so you can now simulate shutting off certain systems such as the fuel, magnetos and electrics, as long as the flaps are not electrically operated. Turn onto finals and deploy flap as required to get you in safely.

As this is only an exercise, we open the throttle to make sure we do not go any lower than 500 feet above the ground and select carb heat to cold. Just adopt the normal go-around procedure and climb back up to your required height.

Chapter 21

Low Level Flying

Low level flying can be said to occur when the aircraft is at a height of 500 feet above ground or less. Take-off and approach to land do not count. What does count is flying low due to being caught out by low cloud, or inspecting a field in preparation for a forced landing with power. There are also certain VFR Entry and Exit lanes that may require you to fly at low level.

Obstacle Clearance

Good flight planning should have made you aware of any tall obstacles that could conflict with your proposed route. When descending to low level you will notice that your field of view becomes limited. Therefore, you should be ready to recognise and avoid any potentially hazardous structures.

Charts and maps give heights of obstacles as above mean sea level, so remember to set your altimeter to the correct local area QNH.

Effect of Wind

At low level the effect of wind speed and direction become much more apparent. Head and Tail winds may give you a false impression of your airspeed, so check the ASI for verification.

Likewise, a crosswind will appear to increase your perceived drift over the ground. This could lead to you questioning the balance of the aircraft. So verify using the balance ball on the Turn Co-ordinator.

Be aware also that at low level, turbulence and wind-shear can cause the speed and direction of the wind to change quickly. A good technique is to keep one hand on the throttle in case quick changes of power become necessary.

One final point, remember to consult the rules pertaining to low flying before practicing this exercise.

Chapter 22

Precautionary Landings

The Precautionary Search and Landing

Having to land at an unfamiliar aerodrome or even in a field may be due to several reasons. The pilot may become ill, forcing him or her to land early, there could be problems because of bad weather or the onset of darkness.

Make your decision early and then look for a suitable landing site. Use the five "Ss" as detailed in the last section.

Let an ATS unit know your intentions as soon as possible. If you cannot communicate with the local unit, re-tune the radio to 121.5 and try again.

If no ATC response, retune to 121.5

Although each situation will be different, the following technique can act as a guide.

For the purposes of this exercise, we'll assume a low cloud-base, with darkness approaching and no airfield within range.

Ok, a possible landing strip has been identified, so descend from the present height to 500 feet above ground in order to reach the threshold of the landing area at that height.

Decide on a suitable landing area

At the same time, select one stage of flap. This will allow us to fly at a slower speed making the first visual inspection easier.

Line the aircraft up just to the right of the landing strip so a clear view is obtained.

At this point, it's a good idea to turn the Direction Indicator to "0" and align it with the strip. This will help when you come around again.

Adjust the DI to "0" degrees when aligned to landing strip

As we fly up the landing area, look out for any obstacles, ditches, fences or anything that could pose a hazard. At the end of the run, stay at 500 feet if it is safe to do so.

Ok, we're approaching our turn onto finals again for a second inspection and now we descend to 200 feet above the ground. The first stage of flap is still deployed. As an additional safety factor, trim the aircraft so it is slightly nose high. This will help stop any tendency to descend further whilst your attention is out of the cockpit.

This time inspect the surface more closely; any there any large rocks, potholes or other hazards. At the end, add power and climb back to 500 feet.

After two inspections, we're happy to attempt a landing, so complete all the pre-landing checks as normal.

On base leg, lower the second stage of flap.

Turn onto final, deploy full flap and approach as if to make a short or soft field landing so as not to overstress the aircraft.

However, since this is an exercise, employ the go-around procedure and climb back to your desired altitude.

Ditching in Water

If ditching in water should ever become necessary, make a MAYDAY call as soon as possible and squawk 7700 on the transponder.

Make a Mayday call & squawk 7700

If the water is smooth or has a very long swell, land into wind.

If there is a large swell running or the water is rough, then try to land along the swell; you must try to avoid hitting the swell head on.

Aim to land with a small amount of flap deployed and with a low airspeed. The attitude should be nose high and a slow rate of descent controlled by power. Do not stall the aircraft.

You should expect two impacts; the first will be the tail hitting the water followed by a much larger impact of the nose hitting the water.

Ideally, you would already be wearing a life-jacket, but do not inflate it until you are clear of the aircraft. Inflation inside could easily hamper your escape.

Chapter 23

Pilot Navigation

This section covers the practical application of pilot navigation; you should consult an approved publication for a more detailed appraisal.

Navigation starts with flight planning

Pilot navigation falls into two categories, flight planning and en-route navigation. Remember, the better the flight planning, the easier the en-route navigation; an important point when you are also concerned with flying the aircraft as well.

Flight planning starts with checking the weather on route to see if the flight will be possible. Actual weather and forecasts can often be obtained from the airfield Briefing Office or from telephone and on-line AIRMET services.

Check the current NOTAMS and AIP for any information that may affect the flight.

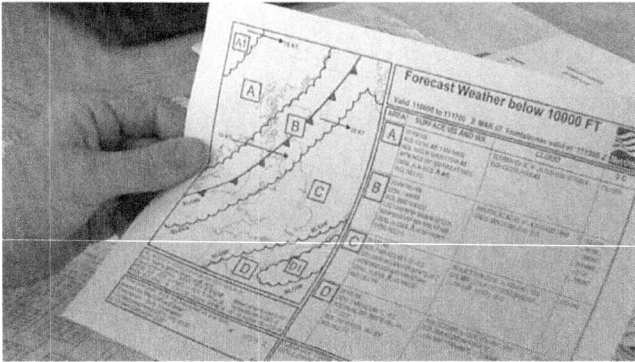

Obtain the latest weather information

The flight log is an effective way of recording all the relevant information that will be needed before and during a flight. To begin entering information, obtain a current ½ million scale chart of the proposed route.

Use a chinagraph or other suitable writing implement to mark out the route and check the safety altitude for each leg. As a guide, the height to fly would be at least 1000 feet above the tallest feature 10 miles either side of track.

Check your track for obstacles

Next, measure the track in degrees True and the distances in nautical miles. Enter these into the log.

Measure distances & headings

Each leg can be broken up into segments of say, 10 miles. This will help with the en-route navigation.

Headings, ground speeds and estimated timings for each leg have to be calculated. The best way is to use a Flight Navigation Computer; your navigation textbook will explain this in detail. These calculations are then added to the log.

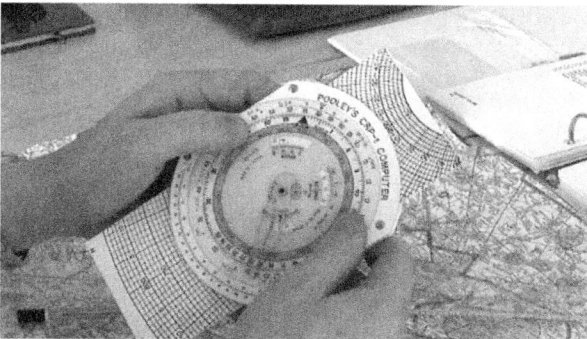

Be adept at using a flight computer

Work out the total estimated time for the flight and obtain the fuel consumption figures from the Flight Manual. The fuel required can then be worked out.

However, the published figures refer to an engine that has been leaned out correctly, so air on the side of caution. In addition you should add a reserve of fuel equal to at least another 45 minutes in the air. But it is wise to allow plenty of extra fuel just in case.

Before any flight it is important to know that the aircraft is not overweight or that the centre of gravity has not moved out of its safe limits. This is known as the Weight and Balance. If in doubt, complete a Load Sheet for your particular aircraft.

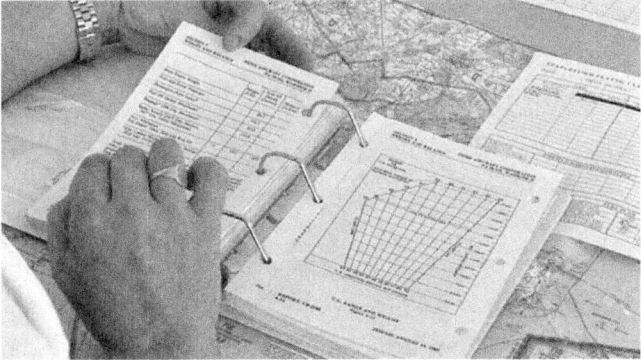

Check your weight & balance tables

All of these factors have a direct effect on the Performance of an aircraft. If in any doubt, check the Performance Tables in your Flight Manual.

Always check the aircraft documents

There are also documents pertaining to the aircraft which have to be checked to see if the aircraft is legal to fly. These include the Certificate of Airworthiness and the Maintenance Schedule.

Finally, remember to "Book Out"; the procedure for this will vary from airfield to airfield.

After taking off, you ideally need to set your initial heading and the clock when overhead the airfield. This may not always be possible, so you should be prepared to make an educated estimate as you leave the circuit.

Set your clock overhead the airfield if possible

Remember to request the QNH and set it on the altimeter subscale.

Set the current QNH

As you begin the en-route phase of the exercise, arrange the chart to read in the direction you are heading. Then re-align the DI with the compass.

Align the DI with the compass

Try to anticipate the ground features before you see them. This means reading the map first and then looking out in order to confirm your position.

Read the map first then look out to confirm features

At periods throughout the flight carry out the FREDA check for your particular aircraft.

It is unusual for a flight to run exactly as planned; the direction and speed of the wind can change necessitating the need to alter your heading in order to compensate. You must also be prepared to keep revising your ETA.

If you should go off track, there are a number of accepted corrections to get you back on. It is best to decide on one with the help of your flying instructor.

As you approach a turning point, check that the DI is in agreement with the compass and make your turn overhead the point.

At different times and depending on your route, you may have to contact various ATS units in order to request the QNH, give position reports or seek permission to fly through certain zones. These frequencies should be in your flight log.

If possible, talk to the ATS unit at your destination about 10 minutes before arrival. This will give you adequate time to plan your approach and landing in line with the current circuit pattern.

Make a normal landing and remember to "book in" at the new airfield.

There may be times when you become uncertain of your present position; this does not necessarily mean that you are lost. The first thing to do is record your heading using both the DI and compass and log the time.

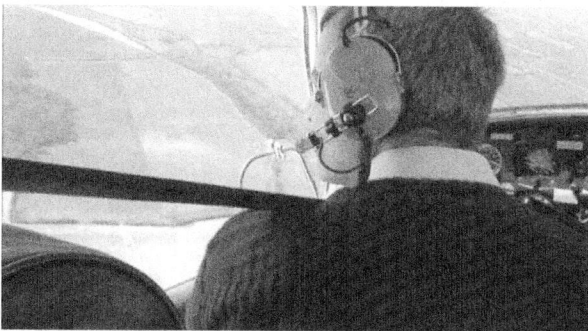

You may become unsure of your position

If the DI and compass are not in agreement, note the difference and re-align them. This should be enough information to estimate your present position.

If the compass and DI are in agreement, then it's possible that a route feature has been misread. Look from map to ground and try to recognise any other prominent features.

If still unsure make an Urgency call

After a short while, if you are still uncertain of your position, then make an Urgency Call on 121.5. They should be able to fix your position, so that you can continue your own navigation.

On the other hand, if you are convinced you are lost from the start make the Urgency Call first to obtain a Radar Fix.

If you are unable to make contact with ATC, look at the chart and mark the position of your last positive fix. Then check the heading that has been flown since.

Check also that there are no metal objects near the compass and that it aligns with the DI.

Next check that the magnetic variation and drift have been applied correctly.

Check for metal objects near the compass

If no obvious errors are found, start to read the chart but this time read it from ground to map. Look for prominent ground features in the general direction of travel.

Try to establish an area where you are likely to be. Draw lines 30 degrees either side of track, fanning out from your last fix.

If this is unsuccessful, consider climbing higher for a better view or aim in the direction of a major feature within range, like a coastline in order to get a fix.

Climb higher & look for larger features

If all else fails, consider making a precautionary search and landing as outlined in the relevant Section.

Chapter 24

Using the Flight Instruments

A pilot flying visually uses the horizon as his attitude reference, whereas a pilot flying on instruments uses the Attitude Indicator and Tachometer as his control instruments. The basic flight instruments are normally arranged in a T-bar shape.

Flight instruments

The Attitude Indicator or AI is the master instrument and provides pitch and bank angle information.

Attitude indicator

The Airspeed Indicator or ASI not only shows the airspeed, it can also act as a back-up to the AI by providing information on whether the nose is high or low for the selected power setting.

Airspeed indicator

The Altimeter indicates height but can also provide pitch information by showing increases or decreases in height.

Altimeter

The Vertical Speed Indicator or VSI provides information on steady rates of climb or descent. But it can also help to back-up the Altimeter and ASI.

Vertical speed indicator

Each of the above instruments is pressure operated, so expect them to exhibit some lag.

The Turn Co-ordinator is a gyroscopic instrument, electrically operated and shows the rate and direction of a turn.

It also contains a balance ball which is controlled using the rudder pedals.

Turn co-ordinator

The Direction Indicator or DI shows the magnetic heading of the aircraft and has to be periodically aligned with the compass.

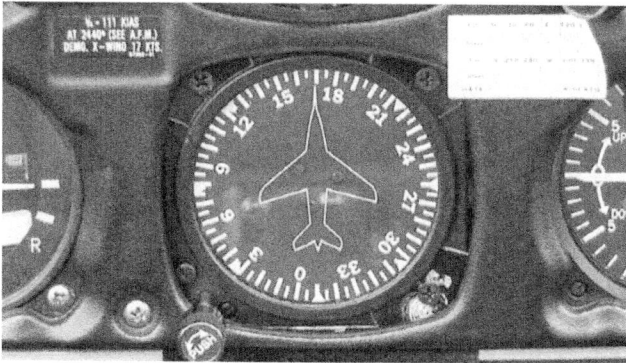

Direction indicator

The Instrument Scan is the means by which the pilot can observe the relevant instruments during any particular phase of a flight.

Flying Straight and Level on Instruments

Establishing Straight and Level Flight

To establish the aircraft for straight and level flight, first select the correct power setting.

Then set the pitch attitude for level flight by positioning the aircraft index on the artificial horizon of the AI.

Hold the attitude and allow the aircraft to settle.

Now, conduct your instrument scan as follows;-

Instrument scan

AI – ALT – AI - VSI – AI - DI – AI – ASI – AI – TC – AI – ALT - etc.

Raising the Nose at Constant Power

To raise the nose at constant power, move the aircraft index on the AI to a point just above the artificial horizon.

The ASI will decrease to a lower value.

186

The ASI will decrease

The altimeter shows an increase in height and the VSI will settle on a steady rate of climb.

Lowering the Nose at Constant Power

To lower the nose at constant power, place the aircraft index of the AI at a position slightly lower than the horizon bar.

ASI increases, altimeter decreases and VSI shows steady rate of descent

The ASI shows a gradual increase in speed.

The altimeter shows decreasing height and the VSI indicates a steady rate of descent.

Maintaining Straight and Level Flight at Constant Power

To maintain straight and level flight at constant power, use the instrument scan already outlined;-

AI – ALT – AI – VSI – AI - DI – AI – ASI – AI – TC – AI – ALT – etc.

To make small changes in altitude, make small corrections on the AI and trim.

Use small bank inputs to maintain heading

If the heading wanders, apply a small amount of bank and balance with rudder.

Adjust airspeed with small changes in power

A change in airspeed can be corrected by adjusting the power with throttle and then altering the attitude slightly to compensate.

Changing Airspeed in Straight and Level Flight

To increase speed at a constant height, add power, balance with rudder input and apply forward pressure on the control column.

Slowly lower the pitch angle to avoid climbing until the new airspeed is reached.

Then adjust the power to maintain the new speed and re-trim.

To decrease airspeed at a constant height, reduce the power, balance with rudder input and lift the nose so as not to descend.

Continue slowly raising the nose until the new airspeed is reached; then adjust the power to maintain the desired speed. Finally, re-trim the aircraft.

Climb, Cruise and Descend at Constant Airspeed

In this exercise, we're going to climb, cruise and then descend using only the flight instruments. Normally, each phase would require a different airspeed, so to make things simple, we will keep the speed constant.

At present, the aircraft is in straight and level flight.

Note the airspeed and then open the throttle to full power and balance with rudder.

Open the throttle to full power and balance with rudder

Allow the nose to rise slightly in order to maintain airspeed. Hold the attitude.

Notice that the VSI is showing a positive rate of climb and the altimeter is indicating increasing height.

Altimeter increases and VSI shows positive rate of climb

When steady, trim the aircraft.

To level off, lower the nose and reduce power to maintain airspeed. Balance with rudder.

Now the VSI reads zero and the altimeter is constant.

Altimeter constant & VSI reads zero

Next, we're going to commence a descent. So, reduce power, balance again with rudder and lower the nose just enough to maintain airspeed.

The VSI now shows a descent and the altimeter is decreasing. When steady, re-trim the aircraft.

Altimeter now decreases & VSI shows a descent

Finally, we're going to enter a climb directly from this descent.

Smoothly go to full power, balance with rudder and at the same time allow the nose to rise to the climb attitude.

Hold this attitude in order to maintain the airspeed.

The VSI is now showing a positive rate of climb and the altimeter is rising.

Altimeter increasing & VSI shows positive rate of climb

Once again, when steady, trim the aircraft.

Initiating a Climb at Normal Climb Speed

We're about to start a climb at normal climb speed from a straight and level attitude. Note the airspeed and increase power to the climb setting and balance with rudder. Raise the nose to the correct pitch attitude for the climb and hold it until the airspeed decreases to the desired climbing speed.

Raise the nose to the correct pitch attitude

The VSI shows a positive rate of climb and the altimeter is increasing.

Use small adjustments in pitch to maintain the correct speed. When steady, trim.

Levelling Off from a Climb

In order to level off at a desired altitude, lower the nose to the cruise position and note the VSI trend. Allow the airspeed to increase to the cruise figure.

Then reduce the power to the cruise setting and make minor adjustments to maintain height, heading and airspeed.

Monitor your height, heading & airspeed

Then, trim the aircraft.

Initiating a Descent on Instruments

To start a descent on instruments, first reduce power, balance and hold the attitude steady in order to maintain height.

The airspeed drops back to the desired descent speed. As it does, lower the nose to maintain this speed.

Lower the nose to maintain your desired airspeed

VSI = rate of descent and Alt indicates decreasing height.

VSI shows a rate of descent

Adjust airspeed with elevators and descent rate with power.

Adjust your airspeed with elevator input

Trim the aircraft.

Controlling the Rate of Descent at a Constant Airspeed

To increase the rate of descent, reduce power and lower the nose to maintain the airspeed.

If you wish to decrease the rate of descent, increase power and raise the nose in order to maintain the airspeed.

In both cases, you should monitor the VSI as a measure of your rate of descent. An alternative would be using the altimeter and stopwatch together.

Monitor your rate of descent

Levelling Off from a Descent

To level off from a descent, first anticipate your desired level-off altitude and increase power. Balance with rudder and raise the nose to the cruise attitude.

Maintain altitude with minor adjustments and re-trim.

Climbing Away from a Descent

To climb away from a descent, apply climb power, balance with rudder and select the correct climb attitude.

Select the correct climb attitude

When steady, trim the aircraft.

Turning Using the Flight Instruments

Rate 1 Turn

We're going to make a level Rate 1 turn solely using the flight instruments.

Remember, you can work out your bank angle by dividing your speed in knots by 10 and then add 7.

So, if your speed is 100 knots, the bank angle would be 10 + 7 = 17 degrees.

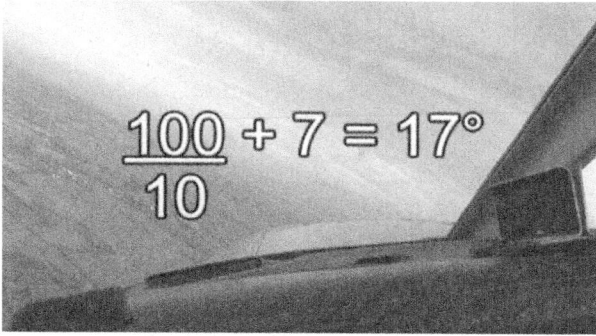

Calculating bank angle

Ok, roll the aircraft to the required bank angle using ailerons and balance with the rudder. Use the elevators to maintain the correct pitch. Confirm using the VSI.

The Rate 1 indicator on the Turn Co-ordinator means we are turning at 3 degrees every second or 360 degrees every 2 minutes.

Rate 1 turn as indicated on the turn co-ordinator

Alternatively, we can work out our turn using the DI and the stopwatch.

To turn out, anticipate the desired heading by about 5 degrees and roll the wings level. Balance with rudder input and lower the nose to the position necessary for straight and level flight.

The 30 Degree Banked Level Turn

We're presently at a bank angle of 30 degrees. This angle may not be easy to distinguish on the turn co-ordinator, so use the AI instead.

The AI can be used to monitor bank angle

Notice that since more back pressure is required, the ASI is slightly lower than that of a Rate 1 turn.

The Climbing Turn

Let's take a look at the climbing turn. In general, try not to exceed a bank angle of 20 degrees.

Notice that both the AI and turn co-ordinator can be used.

Both AI & turn co-ordinator can be used

The instrument scan shows that the altimeter is increasing, the VSI indicates a steady positive rate of climb and the DI is showing our direction of turn.

Lower the nose to maintain desired airspeed

The nose has been lowered in order to maintain airspeed.

Descending Turns

Finally, we're in a descending turn.

The AI and turn co-ordinator indicate a steady bank angle with the pitch lower than that used in a straight descent.

Altimeter decreasing & VSI shows a steady rate of descent

The altimeter is decreasing and the VSI shows a steady rate of descent.

Airspeed is constant and the DI is indicating the direction of turn.

Recovery from Unusual Attitudes Using Instruments

There are generally two types of unusual attitudes; one where the nose is unusually high and the airspeed reducing and two, where the nose of the aircraft is unusually low and the airspeed increasing.

If the attitude becomes extreme, there is a chance that the master instrument, the AI, will topple and become useless. If that happens, we will need to use other instruments to replace it.

Nose High / Steep Bank

The aircraft has developed an unusual attitude. By referring to the AI, we can see that it is indicating the aircraft is nose high with a steep angle of bank applied.

Nose high/steep bank

The ASI is showing our speed is falling dangerously low; there is the possibility of the aircraft stalling.

The ASI shows the aircraft is close to stalling

To recover, positively lower the nose and at the same time, apply full power and balance with rudder.

When the ASI increases back to a safe speed above the stall, roll the wings level and bring the aircraft back to straight and level flight.

Nose Low / Steep Bank

In a low nose/high airspeed configuration, there is a chance of over-speeding or developing into a spiral dive.

The AI is confirming our attitude and the ASI is increasing towards the danger area.

Nose low/steep bank

To recover, first close the throttle and then roll the wings level.

Start to ease out of the dive and continue easing back until the AI indicates the aircraft is straight and level.

Then add sufficient power either to maintain the desired airspeed or to gain the height you had lost.

This concludes the Private Pilot's Flying Course. Remember to read each section before your flying lesson and when you have your pilot's licence, you can always use this book as an aid memoire.

Enjoy every flight.

Contact

For further information about the author, go to

www.johnpullenwriter.com

For further information about pilot training

and a range of flight training DVDs, go to

www.pilottrainingdvds.com

Other Books by the same Author

Non-Fiction

Aviation Series

How to Fly a Plane

How to Fly an Airliner

The Private Pilot Flying Course

The Private Pilot Skill Test

The Flight Pilot Radio Manual

The Instrument Rating Flying Course

Medical Series

Hypnotherapy

Being Happy

Stop Smoking

History Series

Secret London Churches

Secret London Places

Secret Bloody London

Secret Dead London

Flying the Dream

Fiction

Dragon's Claw

Dark Angel

Rogue Knight

Time Warrior

All available, print & EBook through CreateSpace & Amazon

Search "John Pullen" on

www.createspace.com & www.amazon.co.uk

Printed in Great Britain
by Amazon

65567593R00122